THE WORLD OF ENGLISH: DRAMA

TRAGICAL ⋆ COMICAL
HISTORICAL ⋆ PASTORAL

An Anthology from Shakespeare's Plays

compiled and edited by

LIONEL GOUGH

EDWARD ARNOLD

© LIONEL GOUGH 1959

★

First Published 1959
By Edward Arnold (Publishers) Ltd
41 Bedford Square
London WC1B 3DQ
Reprinted 1959, 1961, 1962, 1964,
1966, 1970, 1973, 1976, 1979

ISBN: 0 7131 1177 1

Printed in Great Britain by
Whitstable Litho Ltd., Whitstable, Kent

TO THE READER

In recent years some teachers have been very 'up-stage' (the right word to use here) about books of snippets, gobbets and — in short — 'bits' from Shakespeare. A play, we have been told, is a Complete Aesthetic Experience, and can be read or seen only in its fullness. No good can be gained from acting a few scenes or reading a few acts.

In fact no bread is better than a slice or two!

This seems to me to be nonsense.

Would you say it was wrong to listen to one record from Handel's *Messiah* without hearing the whole of the oratorio? Would you refuse to look at one episode of a serial play on TV unless you were sure you would be able to see the lot? Have you never watched one or two sets of tennis? or part of a cricket match?

Of course it is more satisfying to hear or see the whole of a work of art, or of a game; but I cling to the old belief that something is better than nothing.

We all know that Shakespeare was a man of the theatre — playwright, actor, and part owner of two theatres — and that he wrote his plays to be acted on stages and not read in classrooms. But theatres are few and far between — and the seats are rather expensive — and not everyone is going to seek out stage productions of Shakespeare — especially if he knows nothing about him except that he is 'classical', and therefore probably rather heavy going.

School teachers have, you see, to lead the horses (that is, you) to the water — in the hope that they may drink. A few draughts of Shakespeare may, I hope, make you want to drink deeper — either by reading a whole play or by watching one on TV, or — best of all — by going to Stratford-on-Avon or the Old Vic or any theatre where one of his plays is being presented. To enjoy one of the arts it will be necessary for you to make room for it in your life: to sacrifice some time, effort and money. Once the taste is created, it goes on growing: you have to satisfy it, and you will satisfy it, and nothing will stop you.

May this book, then, drive you towards the theatre!

There is, however, a further justification for it, and that is that Shakespeare was a poet as well as a dramatist. Some of his speeches can be read outside the plays simply as a series of wonderful ideas wonderfully expressed. Poetry is the language of the imagination. In Shakespeare you meet a man who had the liveliest possible imagination: often when you read of something as Shakespeare describes it you feel that you have never really seen it before, and his words about it will never leave you.

So not only am I in favour of a book of scenes from plays: I am even in favour of those tear-off calendars on which you can find a Gem from Shakespeare for Every Day of the Year. And why not? Isn't your imagination enriched by thinking of the bees as 'the singing masons, building roofs of gold', or of 'the uncertain glory of an April day', or of the winds which

> 'take the ruffian billows by the top,
> Curling their monstrous heads, and hanging them
> With deafening clamour in the slippery clouds
> That, with the hurly, death itself awakes'?

Of course it is. I once came across a boy who took to Shakespeare because he had been turning over the leaves of the *Oxford Dictionary of Quotations* and, coming on the 'bits' from Shakespeare, had thought 'What grand stuff this is!'

So I am quite unrepentant about my selection of Great Moments from the Bard: it is for your enjoyment.

LIONEL GOUGH

CONTENTS

MURDER AT INVERNESS CASTLE   7

A POUND OF FLESH   23

ON THE ENCHANTED ISLAND   41

DETERMINED TO PROVE A VILLAIN   64

DOOM OF DICTATOR   82

RIOT IN THE FORUM   94

FALSTAFF IN GLOUCESTERSHIRE   106

ALARUMS AND EXCURSIONS   127

THE EVE OF AGINCOURT   136

ADMIRABLE FOOLING   149

VERY TRAGICAL MIRTH   168

ACKNOWLEDGMENTS

TEXT

Basically that prepared for A. H. Bullen for the Shakespeare Head Stratford Town Shakespeare 1904-1907. Further revised in 1935 for the Shakespeare Head Press Shakespeare published by Basil Blackwell. Alterations usually based on the text and notes of The New Cambridge Shakespeare, *edited by John Dover Wilson.*

PHOTOGRAPHS

Grateful acknowledgment is made to London Film Productions Ltd. and Independent Film Distributors for the still of Sir Laurence Olivier as Richard III and Miss Claire Bloom as Lady Anne, from the film production of Richard III, *and to Mr. John Vickers for the photograph of Sir Ralph Richardson as Falstaff in the Old Vic Theatre Company production of* Henry IV.

MURDER AT INVERNESS CASTLE

Macbeth, hitherto a brave and honourable soldier, has been told by three witches that he is destined to be Thane of Glamis, Thane of Cawdor, and eventually King of Scotland. The first two predictions have come true, and Macbeth's thoughts turn towards the third. Unexpectedly the kind and generous old King Duncan decides to stay the night at Macbeth's castle. With him is a party of his nobles, among whom is the loyal and honest Banquo, to whom the witches have foretold that although he is not to be a king himself, he will be the father of kings. Macbeth's ruthless and ambitious wife determines that this chance of seizing the crown by force must not be missed.

1

Inverness. A room in Macbeth's castle. Enter Lady Macbeth alone, with a letter.

LADY MACBETH   [*Reads*]

1   'THEY met me in the day of success; and I have learn'd
     by the perfect'st report they have more in them than
     mortal knowledge. When I burnt in desire to question
     them further, they made themselves air, into which they
     vanish'd. Whiles I stood rapt in the wonder of it, came
     missives from the king, who all-hail'd me "Thane of
     Cawdor"; by which title, before, these weird sisters
     saluted me, and referr'd me to the coming-on of time,
     with "Hail, king that shalt be!" This have I thought
10   good to deliver thee, my dearest partner of greatness,
     that thou mightst not lose the dues of rejoicing, by being
     ignorant of what greatness is promised thee. Lay it to
     thy heart, and farewell.'
     Glamis thou art, and Cawdor, and shalt be

---

l. 1 *They*: The witches.   l. 10 *deliver*: tell.
l. 6 *missives*: messengers.

What thou art promis'd: yet do I fear thy nature;
It is too full o' th' milk of human kindness
To catch the nearest way: thou wouldst be great;
Art not without ambition; but without
The illness should attend it: what thou wouldst highly,
20   That wouldst thou holily; wouldst not play false,
And yet wouldst wrongly win: thou'ldst have, great Glamis,
That which cries 'Thus thou must do, if thou have it;
And that which rather thou dost fear to do
Than wishest should be undone.' Hie thee hither,
That I may pour my spirits in thine ear;
And chastise with the valour of my tongue
All that impedes thee from the golden round,
Which fate and metaphysical aid doth seem
To have thee crown'd withal.

Enter a Messenger.

What is your tidings?

MESSENGER

30   The king comes here to-night.

LADY MACBETH

Thou'rt mad to say it:
Is not thy master with him? who, were 't so,
Would have inform'd for preparation.

MESSENGER

So please you, it is true: — our thane is coming:
One of my fellows had the speed of him;
Who, almost dead for breath, had scarcely more
Than would make up his message.

LADY MACBETH

Give him tending;
He brings great news.   [*Exit Messenger.*
The raven himself is hoarse

---

l. 19 *illness should*: wickedness   l. 28   *metaphysical*: super-
which should.   natural.

That croaks the fatal entrance of Duncan
Under my battlements. Come, you spirits
40 That tend on mortal thoughts, unsex me here;
And fill me, from the crown to the toe, top-full
Of direst cruelty! make thick my blood,
Stop up th' access and passage to remorse,
That no compunctious visitings of nature
Shake my fell purpose, nor keep peace between
Th' effect and it! Come to my woman's breasts,
And take my milk for gall, you murd'ring ministers,
Wherever in your sightless substances
You wait on nature's mischief! Come, thick night,
50 And pall thee in the dunnest smoke of hell,
That my keen knife see not the wound it makes,
Nor heaven peep through the blanket of the dark,
To cry 'Hold, hold!'

Enter Macbeth.

          Great Glamis! worthy Cawdor!
Greater than both by the all-hail hereafter!
Thy letters have transported me beyond
This ignorant present, and I feel now
The future in the instant.

MACBETH

          My dearest love,
Duncan comes here to-night.

LADY MACBETH

          And when goes hence?

MACBETH

To-morrow, as he purposes.

LADY MACBETH

          O, never
60 Shall sun that morrow see!

---

l. 40 *mortal*: murderous.   l. 45 *keep peace between*: inter-
fere between.

Your face, my thane, is as a book where men
May read strange matters: — to beguile the time
Look like the time; bear welcome in your eye,
Your hand, your tongue: look like the innocent flower,
But be the serpent under't. He that's coming
Must be provided for: and you shall put
This night's great business into my dispatch;
Which shall to all our nights and days to come
Give solely sovereign sway and masterdom.

MACBETH

70 We will speak further.

LADY MACBETH

　　　　　Only look up clear;
To alter favour ever is to fear:
Leave all the rest to me.

2

*Before Macbeth's castle. Enter Duncan, Malcolm, Donalbain,
Banquo, Lennox, Macduff, Ross, Angus and Attendants.*

DUNCAN

1 THIS castle hath a pleasant seat; the air
Nimbly and sweetly recommends itself
Unto our gentle senses.

BANQUO

　　　　　This guest of summer,
The temple-haunting martlet, does approve,
By his lov'd mansionry, that the heavens' breath
Smells wooingly here: no jutty, frieze,
Buttress, nor coign of vantage, but this bird

---

l. 62 *beguile the time*: deceive
the world.
l. 70 *clear*: cheerfully.
l. 71 *alter favour*: change
countenance.

l. 3 *gentle*: peaceful.
l. 4 *martlet*: house-martin.
l. 4 *approve*: prove.
l. 7 *coign of vantage*: convenient corner.

Hath made his pendent bed and procreant cradle:
Where they most breed and haunt I have observ'd
10 The air is delicate.

Enter Lady Macbeth.

DUNCAN

See, see, our honour'd hostess!
The love that follows us sometime is our trouble
Which still we thank as love. Herein I teach you
How you shall bid God 'ild us for your pains,
And thank us for your trouble.

LADY MACBETH

All our service
In every point twice done, and then done double,
Were poor and single business to contend
Against those honours deep and broad wherewith
Your majesty loads our house: for those of old,
And the late dignities heap'd up to them,
20 We rest your hermits.

DUNCAN

Where's the thane of Cawdor?
We cours'd him at the heels, and had a purpose
To be his purveyor: but he rides well;
And his great love, sharp as his spur, hath holp him
To his home before us. Fair and noble hostess,
We are your guest to-night.

LADY MACBETH

Your servants ever
Have theirs, themselves, and what is theirs, in compt,
To make their audit at your highness' pleasure,
Still to return your own.

---

l. 8 *procreant*: for breeding.
l. 13 *'ild*: reward.
l. 16 *single*: feeble.
l. 20 *rest your hermits*: shall pray for you.

l. 22 *purveyor*: fore-runner.
l. 26 *compt*: trust.
l. 27 *make their audit*: account for.

DUNCAN

Give me your hand;
Conduct me to mine host: we love him highly,
30 And shall continue our graces towards him.
By your leave, hostess.   [*Exeunt.*

3

In the castle. Enter Macbeth.

MACBETH

1 IF it were done — when 'tis done — then 'twere well
It were done quickly: if th' assassination
Could trammel up the consequence, and catch,
With his surcease, success; that but this blow
Might be the be-all and the end-all here,
But here, upon this bank and shoal of time,
We'ld jump the life to come. But in these cases
We still have judgement here; that we but teach
Bloody instructions, which, being taught, return
10 To plague th' inventor: this even-handed justice
Commends th' ingredients of our poison'd chalice
To our own lips. He's here in double trust:
First, as I am his kinsman and his subject,
Strong both against the deed; then, as his host,
Who should against his murderer shut the door,
Not bear the knife myself. Besides, this Duncan
Hath borne his faculties so meek, hath been
So clear in his great office, that his virtues

l. 1 *done*: all over.
l. 3 *trammel up*: net.
l. 4 *surcease*: death.
l. 6 *bank and shoal of time* (in
the ocean of eternity).
l. 7 *jump*: risk.

l. 8 *here*: in this world.
l. 10 *even-handed*: fair-dealing.
l. 11 *ingredients*: mixture.
l. 17 *faculties*: powers.
l. 18 *clear*: blameless.

Will plead like angels, trumpet-tongued, against
20 The deep damnation of his taking-off;
And pity, like a naked new-born babe,
Striding the blast, or heaven's cherubin, hors'd
Upon the sightless couriers of the air,
Shall blow the horrid deed in every eye,
That tears shall drown the wind. I have no spur
To prick the sides of my intent, but only
Vaulting ambition, which o'erleaps itself,
And falls on th' other.

Enter Lady Macbeth.

How now! what news?

LADY MACBETH

He has almost supp'd: why have you left the chamber?

MACBETH

30 Hath he ask'd for me?

LADY MACBETH

Know you not he has?

MACBETH

We will proceed no further in this business:
He hath honour'd me of late; and I have bought
Golden opinions from all sorts of people,
Which would be worn now in their newest gloss,
Not cast aside so soon.

LADY MACBETH

Was the hope drunk
Wherein you dress'd yourself? hath it slept since?
And wakes it now, to look so green and pale
At what it did so freely? From this time
Such I account thy love. Art thou afeard
40 To be the same in thine own act and valour

---

l. 20 *taking-off*: murder.   l. 34 *gloss*: look.
l. 23 *the sightless couriers of the
air*: the winds.

As thou art in desire? Wouldst thou have that
Which thou esteem'st the ornament of life,
And live a coward in thine own esteem,
Letting 'I dare not' wait upon 'I would,'
Like the poor cat i' th' adage?

MACBETH

               Prithee, peace:
I dare do all that may become a man;
Who dares do more is none.

LADY MACBETH

                  What beast was't, then
That made you break this enterprise to me?
When you durst do it, then you were a man;
50 And, to be more than what you were, you would
Be so much more the man. Nor time nor place
Did then adhere, and yet you would make both:
They have made themselves, and that their fitness **now**
Does unmake you. I have given suck, and know
How tender 'tis to love the babe that milks me:
I would, while it was smiling in my face,
Have pluck'd my nipple from his boneless gums,
And dash'd the brains out, had I so sworn as you
Have done to this.

MACBETH

If we should fail?

LADY MACBETH

                      We fail?
60 But screw your courage to the sticking-place,
And we'll not fail. When Duncan is asleep, —
Whereto the rather shall his day's hard journey
Soundly invite him, — his two chamberlains

---

l. 45 *adage*: maxim (the cat
would like to catch fish without
getting its paws wet).

l. 48 *break*: reveal.
l. 52 *adhere*: suit.

Will I with wine and wassail so convince,
That memory, the warder of the brain,
Shall be a fume, and the receipt of reason
A limbeck only: when in swinish sleep
Their drenched natures lie as in a death,
What cannot you and I perform upon
70 Th' unguarded Duncan? what not put upon
His spongy officers, who shall bear the guilt
Of our great quell?

MACBETH

        Bring forth men-children only;
For thy undaunted mettle should compose
Nothing but males. Will it not be received,
When we have mark'd with blood those sleepy two
Of his own chamber, and us'd their very daggers,
That they have done 't?

LADY MACBETH

        Who dares receive it other,
As we shall make our griefs and clamour roar
Upon his death?

MACBETH

       I am settled, and bend up
80 Each corporal agent to this terrible feat.
Away, and mock the time with fairest show:
False face must hide what the false heart doth know.

[*Exeunt.*

4

In the courtyard. Enter Banquo, and Fleance with a torch.

BANQUO

1 How goes the night, boy?

---

l. 64 *wassail*: revelry.   l. 67 *limbeck*: vessel.
l. 64 *convince*: overpower.   l. 71 *spongy*: drunken.
l. 66 *receipt*: container.

FLEANCE

The moon is down; I have not heard the clock.

BANQUO

And she goes down at twelve.

FLEANCE

       I take 't 'tis later, sir.

BANQUO

Hold, take my sword: — there's husbandry in heaven,
Their candles are all out: — take thee that too.
A heavy summons lies like lead upon me,
And yet I would not sleep: — merciful powers,
Restrain in me the cursed thoughts that nature
Gives way to in repose! — Give me my sword. —
10 Who's there?

   Enter Macbeth, and a Servant with a torch.

MACBETH

A friend.

BANQUO

What, sir, not yet at rest? The king's a-bed:
He hath been in unusual pleasure, and
Sent forth great largess to your officers:
This diamond he greets your wife withal,
By the name of most kind hostess; and shut up
In measureless content.

MACBETH

     Being unprepared,
Our will became the servant to defect;
Which else should free have wrought.

BANQUO

        All's well.

---

l. 4 *husbandry*: thrift.
l. 14 *largess*: gifts.
l. 17 *Being unprepared, Our will became the servant to defect;*

Which else should free have wrought: Being unready, we could not entertain the King as well as we should wish.

20 I dreamt last night of the three weird sisters:
To you they have show'd some truth.

MACBETH

I think not of them:
Yet, when we can entreat an hour to serve,
We would spend it in some words upon that business,
If you would grant the time.

BANQUO

At your kind'st leisure.

MACBETH

If you shall cleave to my consent, — when 'tis,
It shall make honour for you.

BANQUO

So I lose none
In seeking to augment it, but still keep
My bosom franchis'd, and allegiance clear,
I shall be counsell'd.

MACBETH

Good repose the while!

BANQUO

30 Thanks, sir: the like to you!

[*Exeunt Banquo and Fleance.*

MACBETH

Go bid thy mistress, when my drink is ready,
She strike upon the bell. Get thee to bed.

[*Exit Servant.*

Is this a dagger which I see before me,
The handle toward my hand? Come, let me clutch
thee: —
I have thee not, and yet I see thee still.

---

l. 25 *cleave to my consent*: take
my side.
l. 25 *'tis*: the time comes.

l. 27 *augment*: increase.
l. 28 *franchis'd*: free.
l. 29 *counsell'd*: do as you say.

Art thou not, fatal vision, sensible
To feeling as to sight? or art thou but
A dagger of the mind, a false creation,
Proceeding from the heat-oppressed brain?
40 I see thee yet, in form as palpable
As this which now I draw.
Thou marshall'st me the way that I was going;
And such an instrument I was to use.
Mine eyes are made the fools o' th' other senses,
Or else worth all the rest: I see thee still;
And on thy blade and dudgeon gouts of blood,
Which was not so before. — There's no such thing:
It is the bloody business which informs
Thus to mine eyes. — Now o'er the one half-world
50 Nature seems dead, and wicked dreams abuse
The curtain'd sleep; now witchcraft celebrates
Pale Hecate's offerings; and wither'd murder,
Alarum'd by his sentinel, the wolf,
Whose howl's his watch, thus with his stealthy pace,
With Tarquin's ravishing strides, towards his design
Moves like a ghost. — Thou sure and firm-set earth,
Hear not my steps, which way they walk, for fear
Thy very stones prate of my whereabout,
And take the present horror from the time,
60 Which now suits with it. — Whiles I threat, he lives:
Words to the heat of deeds too cold breath gives.

[*A bell rings.*

I go, and it is done; the bell invites me.
Hear it not, Duncan; for it is a knell

---

l. 36 *sensible to feeling as to
sight*: to be felt as well as seen.
l. 40 *palpable*: real.
l. 46 *dudgeon*: hilt.
l. 48 *informs*: takes form.

l. 52 *Hecate's*: Queen of
Witches.
l. 55 *Tarquin's*: a Roman
prince, of bad character.
l. 63 *knell*: death bell.

That summons thee to heaven or to hell.   *[Exit.*
Enter Lady Macbeth.

LADY MACBETH

That which hath made them drunk hath made me bold;
What hath quench'd them hath given me fire. — Hark!
  — Peace!
It was the owl that shriek'd, the fatal bellman,
Which gives the stern'st good-night. — He is about it:
The doors are open; and the surfeited grooms
70   Do mock their charge with snores: I have drugg'd their
    possets,
That death and nature do contend about them,
Whether they live or die.

MACBETH *[within]*
           Who's there? what, ho!

LADY MACBETH

Alack, I am afraid they have awak'd,
And 'tis not done: — th' attempt, and not the deed,
Confounds us. — Hark! — I laid their daggers ready
He could not miss 'em. — Had he not resembled
My father as he slept, I had done 't. — My husband!

Enter Macbeth.

MACBETH

I have done the deed. — Didst thou not hear a noise?

LADY MACBETH

I heard the owl scream and the crickets cry.
80   Did not you speak?

MACBETH
       When?

LADY MACBETH
       Now.

MACBETH
          As I descended?

---

l. 67 *bellman*: crier.   l. 70 *possets*: drinks.

LADY MACBETH

Ay.

MACBETH

Hark! —
Who lies i' th' second chamber?

LADY MACBETH

                    Donalbain.

MACBETH

This is a sorry sight.   [*Looking at his hands.*

LADY MACBETH

A foolish thought, to say a sorry sight.

MACBETH

There's one did laugh in 's sleep, and one cried
  'Murder!'
That they did wake each other: I stood and heard them:
But they did say their prayers, and address'd them
Again to sleep.

LADY MACBETH

        There are two lodg'd together.

MACBETH

90 One cried 'God bless us!' and 'Amen!' the other;
As they had seen me, with these hangman's hands.
Listening their fear, I could not say 'Amen!'
When they did say 'God bless us!'

LADY MACBETH

                Consider it not so deeply.

MACBETH

But wherefore could not I pronounce 'Amen'?
I had most need of blessing, and 'Amen'
Stuck in my throat.

LADY MACBETH

            These deeds must not be thought
After these ways; so, it will make us mad.

20

MACBETH

Methought I heard a voice cry, 'Sleep no more!
Macbeth does murder sleep,' — the innocent sleep,
100 Sleep that knits up the ravell'd sleave of care,
The death of each day's life, sore labour's bath,
Balm of hurt minds, great nature's second course,
Chief nourisher in life's feast, —

LADY MACBETH

What do you mean?

MACBETH

Still it cried 'Sleep no more!' to all the house:
'Glamis hath murder'd sleep, and therefore Cawdor
Shall sleep no more, — Macbeth shall sleep no more!'

LADY MACBETH

Who was it that thus cried? Why, worthy thane,
You do unbend your noble strength, to think
So brainsickly of things. — Go get some water,
110 And wash this filthy witness from your hand. —
Why did you bring these daggers from the place?
They must lie there: go carry them, and smear
The sleepy grooms with blood.

MACBETH

I'll go no more:
I am afraid to think what I have done;
Look on 't again I dare not.

LADY MACBETH

Infirm of purpose!
Give me the daggers: the sleeping and the dead
Are but as pictures: 'tis the eye of childhood
That fears a painted devil. If he do bleed,

---

l. 100 *knits up the ravell'd
sleave*: ties up the tangled
threads.

I'll gild the faces of the grooms withal;

120 For it must seem their guilt.　　　[*Exit. Knock within.*

MACBETH

　　　　　　　Whence is that knocking?
How is 't with me, when every noise appals me?
What hands are here? ha! they pluck out mine eyes!
Will all great Neptune's ocean wash this blood
Clean from my hand? No; this my hand will rather
The multitudinous seas incarnadine,
Making the green one red.

Enter Lady Macbeth.

LADY MACBETH

My hands are of your colour; but I shame
To wear a heart so white. [*Knock.*] I hear a knocking
At the south entry: — retire we to our chamber:

130 A little water clears us of this deed:
How easy is it, then! Your constancy
Hath left you unattended. — [*Knock.*] Hark! more
　　knocking:
Get on your nightgown, lest occasion call us,
And show us to be watchers: — be not lost
So poorly in your thoughts.

MACBETH

To know my deed, 'twere best not know myself.

　　　　　　　　　　　　　　[*Knock.*

Wake Duncan with thy knocking! I would thou couldst!

Macbeth I. 5 — II. 2

---

l. 125 *incarnadine*: turn blood-
red.

A POUND OF FLESH

*Antonio, a Venetian merchant, authorized his friend Bassanio,
who was hard up, to borrow 3000 ducats from the Jew, Shylock.
Longing to revenge himself for the scorn with which he had been
treated, Shylock agreed to lend the money on the fantastic
condition that if it were not repaid in three months he could have
a pound of Antonio's flesh instead. The risk was taken and the
agreement made; but unfortunately Antonio had a series of
heavy losses, and now on settlement day he cannot find the
money. Meanwhile Bassanio has married a wealthy girl named
Portia: her maid Nerissa has married Gratiano, another of
Bassanio's friends. The two women, disguised as a distinguished
lawyer and his clerk, have thought of a plan which may foil the
villain and save Antonio's life.*

A Court of Justice.

DUKE OF VENICE

1 WHAT, is Antonio here?

ANTONIO

Ready, so please your Grace.

DUKE OF VENICE

I am sorry for thee: thou art come to answer
A stony adversary, an inhuman wretch
Uncapable of pity, void and empty
From any dram of mercy.

ANTONIO

     I have heard
Your Grace hath ta'en great pains to qualify
His rigorous course; but since he stands obdurate,
And that no lawful means can carry me
10 Out of his envy's reach, I do oppose
My patience to his fury, and am arm'd

---

l. 7 *qualify*: soften.   l. 8 *obdurate*: relentless.

To suffer, with a quietness of spirit,
The very tyranny and rage of his.

DUKE OF VENICE

Go one, and call the Jew into the court.

SOLANIO

He's ready at the door: he comes, my lord.

Enter Shylock.

DUKE OF VENICE

Make room, and let him stand before our face.
Shylock, the world thinks (and I think so too),
That thou but lead'st this fashion of thy malice
To the last hour of act; and then 'tis thought
20   Thou'lt show thy mercy and remorse more strange
Than is thy strange apparent cruelty;
And where thou now exact'st the penalty, —
Which is a pound of this poor merchant's flesh, —
Thou wilt not only loose the forfeiture,
But, touch'd with human gentleness and love,
Forgive a moiety of the principal;
Glancing an eye of pity on his losses,
That have of late so huddled on his back,
Enow to press a royal merchant down,
30   And pluck commiseration of his state
From brassy bosoms and rough hearts of flint,
From stubborn Turks and Tartars, never train'd
To offices of tender courtesy.
We all expect a gentle answer, Jew.

SHYLOCK

I have possess'd your Grace of what I purpose;

---

l. 18 *fashion*: pretence.
l. 22 *exact'st*: dost demand.
l. 24 *loose*: give up.
l. 24 *forfeiture*: the pound of Antonio's flesh.

l. 26 *moiety*: part.
l. 26 *principal*: the loan of 3000 ducats.
l. 30 *commiseration of*: pity for.
l. 33 *offices*: duties.

And by our holy Sabbath have I sworn
To have the due and forfeit of my bond:
If you deny it, let the danger light
Upon your charter and your city's freedom.
40 You'll ask me, why I rather choose to have
A weight of carrion-flesh than to receive
Three thousand ducats: I'll not answer that;
But say it is my humour: is it answer'd?
What if my house be troubled with a rat,
And I be pleas'd to give ten thousand ducats
To have it ban'd! What, are you answer'd yet?
Some men there are love not a gaping pig;
Some, that are mad if they behold a cat: ...
As there is no firm reason to be render'd,
50 Why he cannot abide a gaping pig;
Why he, a harmless necessary cat; ...
So can I give no reason, nor I will not,
More than a lodg'd hate and a certain loathing
I bear Antonio, that I follow thus
A losing suit against him. Are you answer'd?

BASSANIO

This is no answer, thou unfeeling man,
To excuse the current of thy cruelty.

SHYLOCK

I am not bound to please thee with my answer.

BASSANIO

Do all men kill the things they do not love?

SHYLOCK

60 Hates any man the thing he would not kill?

---

l. 43 *humour*: whim.
l. 46 *ban'd*: poisoned.
l. 47 *gaping pig*: pig's head
served at table.

l. 50 *he*: one man.
l. 55 *losing*: damaging.

BASSANIO

Every offence is not a hate at first.

SHYLOCK

What, would'st thou have a serpent sting thee twice?

ANTONIO

I pray you, think you question with the Jew:
You may as well go stand upon the beach
And bid the main flood bate his usual height;
You may as well use question with the wolf
Why he hath made the ewe bleat for the lamb;
You may as well forbid the mountain pines
To wag their high tops and to make no noise,
70 When they are fretten with the gusts of heaven;
You may as well do any thing most hard,
As seek to soften that, — than which what's harder? —
His Jewish heart: — therefore, I do beseech you,
Make no more offers, use no further means,
But, with all brief and plain conveniency,
Let me have judgement, and the Jew his will.

BASSANIO

For thy three thousand ducats here is six.

SHYLOCK

If every ducat in six thousand ducats
Were in six parts, and every part a ducat,
80 I would not draw them. I would have my bond.

DUKE OF VENICE

How shalt thou hope for mercy, rendering none?

SHYLOCK

What judgement shall I dread, doing no wrong?
You have among you many a purchas'd slave,
Which, like your asses and your dogs and mules,
You use in abject and in slavish parts

---

l. 65 *bate*: lessen. l. 85 *abject*: mean.
l. 70 *fretten*: vexed. l. 85 *parts*: tasks.

Because you bought them: shall I say to you,
Let them be free, marry them to your heirs?
Why sweat they under burdens? let their beds
Be made as soft as yours, and let their palates
90 Be season'd with such viands? You will answer,
The slaves are ours: — so do I answer you:
The pound of flesh, which I demand of him,
Is dearly bought, 'tis mine, and I will have it.
If you deny me, fie upon your law!
There is no force in the decrees of Venice.
I stand for judgement: answer, — shall I have it?

DUKE OF VENICE

Upon my power I may dismiss this court,
Unless Bellario, a learned doctor
Whom I have sent for to determine this,
100 Come here to-day.

SOLANIO

My lord, here stays without
A messenger with letters from the doctor,
New come from Padua.

DUKE OF VENICE

Bring us the letters; call the messenger.

BASSANIO

Good cheer, Antonio! What, man, courage yet!
The Jew shall have my flesh, blood, bones, and all,
Ere thou shalt lose for me one drop of blood.

ANTONIO

I am a tainted wether of the flock,
Meetest for death: the weakest kind of fruit
Drops earliest to the ground; and so let me:
110 You cannot better be employ'd, Bassanio,
Than to live still, and write mine epitaph.

---

l. 98 *doctor*: Doctor of Laws.　　l. 107 *tainted wether*: diseased
l. 99 *determine*: decide.　　sheep.

A POUND OF FLESH

Enter Nerissa, dressed like a lawyer's clerk.

DUKE OF VENICE

Came you from Padua, from Bellario?

NERISSA

From both, my lord. Bellario greets your Grace.

[*Presents a letter.*

BASSANIO

Why dost thou whet thy knife so earnestly?

SHYLOCK

To cut the forfeiture from that bankrout there.

GRATIANO

Not on thy sole, but on thy soul, harsh Jew,
Thou mak'st thy knife keen; but no metal can,
No, not the hangman's axe, bear half the keenness
Of thy sharp envy. Can no prayers pierce thee?

SHYLOCK

120 No, none that thou hast wit enough to make.

GRATIANO

O, be thou damn'd, inexorable dog!
And for thy life let justice be accused.
Thou almost mak'st me waver in my faith,
To hold opinion with Pythagoras
That souls of animals infuse themselves
Into the trunks of men: thy currish spirit
Govern'd a wolf, who, hang'd for human slaughter,
Even from the gallows did his fell soul fleet,
And, whilst thou lay'st in thy unhallow'd dam,
130 Infus'd itself in thee; for thy desires
Are wolfish, bloody, starv'd, and ravenous.

SHYLOCK

Till thou canst rail the seal from off my bond,

---

l. 121 *inexorable*: relentless.
l. 124 *Pythagoras*: a Greek
philosopher.

l. 126 *trunks*: bodies.
l. 128 *fleet*: slip away.

28

Thou but offend'st thy lungs to speak so loud:
Repair thy wit, good youth, or it will fall
To cureless ruin. — I stand here for law.

DUKE OF VENICE

This letter from Bellario doth commend
A young and learned doctor to our court. —
Where is he?

NERISSA

He attendeth here hard by,
To know your answer, whether you'll admit him.

DUKE OF VENICE

140 With all my heart. — Some three or four of you
Go give him courteous conduct to this place. —
Meantime the court shall hear Bellario's letter.

CLERK [reads]

Your Grace shall understand, that at the receipt of your
letter I am very sick: but in the instant that your
messenger came, in loving visitation was with me a young
doctor of Rome; his name is Balthazar. I acquainted
him with the cause in controversy between the Jew and
Antonio the merchant: we turn'd o'er many books
together: he is furnish'd with my opinion; which, better'd
150 with his own learning, — the greatness whereof I cannot
enough commend, — comes with him, at my importunity, to fill up your Grace's request in my stead. I
beseech you, let his lack of years be no impediment to
let him lack a reverend estimation; for I never knew so
young a body with so old a head. I leave him to your
gracious acceptance, whose trial shall better publish his
commendation.

DUKE OF VENICE

You hear the learned Bellario, what he writes:

---

l. 132 *rail*: curse.   l. 151 *importunity*: desire.

And here, I take it, is the doctor come.

Enter Portia disguised as Balthazar.

160 Give me your hand. Come you from old Bellario?

PORTIA

I did, my lord.

DUKE OF VENICE

You are welcome: take your place.
Are you acquainted with the difference
That holds this present question in the court?

PORTIA

I am informed throughly of the cause. —
Which is the merchant here, and which the Jew?

DUKE OF VENICE

Antonio and old Shylock, both stand forth.

PORTIA

Is your name Shylock?

SHYLOCK

Shylock is my name.

PORTIA

Of a strange nature is the suit you follow;
Yet in such rule, that the Venetian law
170 Cannot impugn you as you do proceed. —
You stand within his danger, do you not?

ANTONIO

Ay, so he says.

PORTIA

Do you confess the bond?

ANTONIO

I do.

PORTIA

Then must the Jew be merciful.

---

l. **170** *impugn*: hinder.　　　l. **172** *bond*: bargain.

A POUND OF FLESH

SHYLOCK

On what compulsion must I? tell me that.

PORTIA

The quality of mercy is not strain'd, —
It droppeth as the gentle rain from heaven
Upon the place beneath: it is twice blest, —
It blesseth him that gives, and him that takes:
'Tis mightiest in the mightiest: it becomes
180 The thronèd monarch better than his crown;
His sceptre shows the force of temporal power,
The attribute to awe and majesty,
Wherein doth sit the dread and fear of kings;
But mercy is above this sceptred sway, —
It is enthronèd in the hearts of kings,
It is an attribute to God himself;
And earthly power doth then show likest God's
When mercy seasons justice. Therefore, Jew,
Though justice be thy plea, consider this, —
190 That, in the course of justice, none of us
Should see salvation: we do pray for mercy;
And that same prayer doth teach us all to render
The deeds of mercy. I have spoke thus much
To mitigate the justice of thy plea;
Which if thou follow, this strict court of Venice
Must needs give sentence 'gainst the merchant there.

SHYLOCK

My deeds upon my head! I crave the law,
The penalty and forfeit of my bond.

PORTIA

Is he not able to discharge the money?

---

l. 175 *The quality of mercy is
not strain'd*: A man ought not
to be *compelled* to show mercy.
l. 182 *attribute to*: sign of.
l. 186 *attribute to*: quality of.

l. 188 *seasons*: softens.
l. 194 *mitigate the justice of thy
plea*: ask you to abandon your
legal claim.

BASSANIO

200 Yes, here I tender it for him in the court;
Yea, thrice the sum: if that will not suffice,
I will be bound to pay it ten times o'er,
On forfeit of my hands, my head, my heart:
If this will not suffice, it must appear
That malice bears down truth. And I beseech you,
Wrest once the law to your authority:
To do a great right, do a little wrong;
And curb this cruel devil of his will.

PORTIA

It must not be; there is no power in Venice
210 Can alter a decree established:
'Twill be recorded for a precedent;
And many an error, by the same example,
Will rush into the state: it cannot be.

SHYLOCK

A Daniel come to judgement! yea, a Daniel! —
O wise young judge, how I do honour thee!

PORTIA

I pray you, let me look upon the bond.

SHYLOCK

Here 'tis, most reverend doctor, here it is.

PORTIA

Shylock, there's thrice thy money offer'd thee.

SHYLOCK

An oath, an oath, I have an oath in heaven!
220 Shall I lay perjury upon my soul?
No, not for Venice.

PORTIA

Why, this bond is forfeit;
And lawfully by this the Jew may claim

---

l. 206 *wrest*: twist.
l. 214 *Daniel*: see *The Story of* *Susannah*, an apocryphal book of The Bible.

A pound of flesh, to be by him cut off
Nearest the merchant's heart. — Be merciful:
Take thrice thy money; bid me tear the bond.

SHYLOCK

When it is paid according to the tenour. —
It doth appear you are a worthy judge;
You know the law, your exposition
Hath been most sound: I charge you by the law,
230 Whereof you are a well-deserving pillar,
Proceed to judgement: by my soul I swear
There is no power in the tongue of man
To alter me: I stay here on my bond.

ANTONIO

Most heartily I do beseech the court
To give the judgement.

PORTIA

           Why then, thus it is: —
You must prepare your bosom for his knife.

SHYLOCK

O noble judge! O excellent young man!

PORTIA

For the intent and purpose of the law
Hath full relation to the penalty,
240 Which here appeareth due upon the bond.

SHYLOCK

'Tis very true: O wise and upright judge!
How much more elder art thou than thy looks!

PORTIA

Therefore lay bare your bosom.

SHYLOCK

               Ay, his breast:
So says the bond: — doth it not, noble judge? —
Nearest his heart: those are the very words.

---

l. 226 *tenour*: actual wording.

PORTIA

It is so. Are there balance here to weigh
The flesh?

SHYLOCK

I have them ready.

PORTIA

Have by some surgeon, Shylock, on your charge,
250 To stop his wounds, lest he do bleed to death.

SHYLOCK

Is it so nominated in the bond?

PORTIA

It is not so express'd: but what of that?
'Twere good you do so much for charity.

SHYLOCK

I cannot find it; 'tis not in the bond.

PORTIA

You, merchant, have you any thing to say?

ANTONIO

But little: I am arm'd and well prepared. —
Give me your hand, Bassanio: fare you well!
Grieve not that I am fall'n to this for you;
For herein Fortune shows herself more kind
260 Than is her custom: it is still her use
To let the wretched man outlive his wealth,
To view with hollow eye and wrinkled brow
An age of poverty; from which lingering penance
Of such a misery doth she cut me off.
Commend me to your honourable wife:
Tell her the process of Antonio's end;
Say how I lov'd you, speak me fair in death;
And, when the tale is told, bid her be judge
Whether Bassanio had not once a love.

---

l. 251 *nominated*: laid down.

270 Repent but you that you shall lose your friend,
And he repents not that he pays your debt;
For, if the Jew do cut but deep enough,
I'll pay it presently with all my heart.

BASSANIO

Antonio, I am married to a wife
Which is as dear to me as life itself;
But life itself, my wife, and all the world,
Are not with me esteem'd above thy life:
I would lose all, ay, sacrifice them all
Here to this devil, to deliver you.

PORTIA

280 Your wife would give you little thanks for that,
If she were by, to hear you make the offer.

GRATIANO

I have a wife, whom, I protest, I love:
I would she were in heaven, so she could
Entreat some power to change this currish Jew.

NERISSA

'Tis well you offer it behind her back;
The wish would make else an unquiet house.

SHYLOCK [aside]

These be the Christian husbands! I have a daughter;
Would any of the stock of Barabbas
Had been her husband rather than a Christian! —

290 We trifle time: I pray thee, pursue sentence.

PORTIA

A pound of that same merchant's flesh is thine:
The court awards it, and the law doth give it.

SHYLOCK

Most rightful judge!

PORTIA

And you must cut this flesh from off his breast:
The law allows it, and the court awards it.

SHYLOCK

Most learned judge! — A sentence! come, prepare!

PORTIA

Tarry a little; there is something else.
This bond doth give thee here no jot of blood, —
The words expressly are, 'a pound of flesh':
300 Take then thy bond, take thou thy pound of flesh;
But, in the cutting it, if thou dost shed
One drop of Christian blood, thy lands and goods
Are, by the laws of Venice, confiscate
Unto the state of Venice.

GRATIANO

O upright judge! — Mark, Jew: — O learned judge!

SHYLOCK

Is that the law?

PORTIA

Thyself shalt see the act:
For, as thou urgest justice, be assured
Thou shalt have justice, more than thou desirest.

GRATIANO

O learned judge! — Mark, Jew: — a learned judge!

SHYLOCK

310 I take his offer, then; — pay the bond thrice,
And let the Christian go.

BASSANIO

Here is the money.

PORTIA

Soft!

The Jew shall have all justice; — soft! no haste: —
He shall have nothing but the penalty.

GRATIANO

O Jew! an upright judge, a learned judge!

PORTIA

Therefore prepare thee to cut off the flesh.

Shed thou no blood; nor cut thou less nor more
But just a pound of flesh: if thou cutt'st more
Or less than a just pound, — be it but so much
As makes it light or heavy in the substance,
320 Or the division of the twentieth part
Of one poor scruple, nay, if the scale do turn
But in the estimation of a hair, —
Thou diest, and all thy goods are confiscate.

GRATIANO

A second Daniel, a Daniel, Jew!
Now, infidel, I have you on the hip.

PORTIA

Why doth the Jew pause? take thy forfeiture.

SHYLOCK

Give me my principal, and let me go.

BASSANIO

I have it ready for thee; here it is.

PORTIA

He hath refus'd it in the open court:
330 He shall have merely justice and his bond.

GRATIANO

A Daniel, still say I, a second Daniel! —
I thank thee, Jew, for teaching me that word.

SHYLOCK

Shall I not have barely my principal?

PORTIA

Thou shalt have nothing but the forfeiture,
To be so taken at thy peril, Jew.

SHYLOCK

Why, then the devil give him good of it!
I'll stay no longer question.

---

l. 321 *scruple*: $\frac{1}{24}$ oz.   l. 325 *on the hip*: at a disadvantage (wrestling).

PORTIA

     Tarry, Jew:
The law hath yet another hold on you.
It is enacted in the laws of Venice:
340 If it be prov'd against an alien
That by direct or indirect attempts
He seek the life of any citizen,
The party 'gainst the which he doth contrive
Shall seize one half his goods; the other half
Comes to the privy coffer of the state;
And the offender's life lies in the mercy
Of the duke only, 'gainst all other voice.
In which predicament, I say, thou stand'st;
For it appears, by manifest proceeding,
350 That indirectly, and directly too,
Thou hast contriv'd against the very life
Of the defendant; and thou hast incurr'd
The danger formerly by me rehearsed.
Down, therefore, and beg mercy of the duke.

GRATIANO

Beg that thou mayst have leave to hang thyself:
And yet, thy wealth being forfeit to the state,
Thou hast not left the value of a cord;
Therefore thou must be hang'd at the state's charge.

DUKE OF VENICE

That thou shalt see the difference of our spirits,
360 I pardon thee thy life before thou ask it:
For half thy wealth, it is Antonio's;
The other half comes to the general state,
Which humbleness may drive unto a fine.

PORTIA

Ay, for the state, — not for Antonio.

---

l. 348 *predicament*: situation.   l. 349 *by manifest proceeding*: in open court of law.

SHYLOCK

Nay, take my life and all; pardon not that:
You take my house, when you do take the prop
That doth sustain my house; you take my life,
When you do take the means whereby I live.

PORTIA

What mercy can you render him, Antonio?

GRATIANO

370 A halter gratis; nothing else, for God's sake!

ANTONIO

So please my lord the duke and all the court
To quit the fine for one half of his goods,
I am content; so he will let me have
The other half in use, to render it,
Upon his death, unto the gentleman
That lately stole his daughter:
Two things provided more, — that, for this favour,
He presently become a Christian;
The other, that he do record a gift,
380 Here in the court, of all he dies possess'd,
Unto his son Lorenzo and his daughter.

DUKE OF VENICE

He shall do this; or else I do recant
The pardon that I late pronounced here.

PORTIA

Art thou contented, Jew? what dost thou say?

SHYLOCK

I am content.

PORTIA

Clerk, draw a deed of gift.

SHYLOCK

I pray you, give me leave to go from hence;

---

l. 372 *quit*: excuse him.   l. 378 *presently*: at once.

I am not well: send the deed after me,
And I will sign it.

DUKE OF VENICE
> Get thee gone, but do it.

GRATIANO
In christening shalt thou have two godfathers:
390 Had I been judge, thou shouldst have had ten more,
To bring thee to the gallows, not the font.

> [*Exit Shylock.*

DUKE OF VENICE
Sir, I entreat you home with me to dinner.

PORTIA
I humbly do desire your Grace of pardon:
I must away this night toward Padua,
And it is meet I presently set forth.

DUKE OF VENICE
I am sorry that your leisure serves you not. —
Antonio, gratify this gentleman;
For, in my mind, you are much bound to him.

> [*Exeunt Duke and his Train.*

BASSANIO
Most worthy gentleman, I and my friend
400 Have by your wisdom been this day acquitted
Of grievous penalties; in lieu whereof
Three thousand ducats, due unto the Jew,
We freely cope your courteous pains withal.

ANTONIO
And stand indebted, over and above,
In love and service to you evermore.

PORTIA
He is well paid that is well satisfied;
And I, delivering you, am satisfied,

---

l. 397 *gratify*: reward.   l. 403 *cope*: give in exchange
                                                      for.

And therein do account myself well paid:
My mind was never yet more mercenary.
410 I pray you, know me when we meet again:
I wish you well, and so I take my leave.

The Merchant of Venice, IV. 1

ON THE ENCHANTED ISLAND

Prospero, exiled for some years from his dukedom, is a wizard who can use magic arts and has spirits at his command, of whom the chief is called Ariel. He has lived alone with his beautiful daughter Miranda, served only by a savage and grotesque monster, son of an evil witch. One day a ship containing Prospero's enemies is wrecked on the coast. While Prospero is arranging the marriage of his daughter with the Prince of Naples, the monster Caliban finds allies, also from the ship, who may be able to free him from the enchanter.

1

On the Desert Island, near the shore. Enter Caliban with a burden of wood. A noise of thunder heard.

CALIBAN

1 ALL the infections that the sun sucks up
From bogs, fens, flats, on Prosper fall, and make him
By inch-meal a disease! His spirits hear me,
And yet I needs must curse. But they'll nor pinch,
Fright me with urchin-shows, pitch me i' the mire,

---

l. 3 *inch-meal*: bit by bit.

l. 5 *urchin-shows*: fiends disguised as hedgehogs.

41

Nor lead me, like a firebrand, in the dark
Out of my way, unless he bid 'em: but
For every trifle are they set upon me;
Sometime like apes, that mow and chatter at me,
10 And after bite me; then like hedgehogs, which
Lie tumbling in my barefoot way, and mount
Their pricks at my footfall; sometime am I
All wound with adders, who with cloven tongues
Do hiss me into madness. Lo, now, lo!
Here comes a spirit of his; and to torment me
For bringing wood in slowly. I'll fall flat;
Perchance he will not mind me.

Enter Trinculo, a jester, who has escaped from the wrecked ship.

TRINCULO

Here's neither bush nor shrub, to bear off any weather at
all, and another storm brewing; I hear it sing i' the wind:
20 yond same black cloud, yond huge one, looks like a foul
bombard that would shed his liquor. If it should thunder
as it did before, I know not where to hide my head: yond
same cloud cannot choose but fall by pailfuls. — What
have we here? a man or a fish? dead or alive? A fish: he
smells like a fish; a very ancient and fish-like smell; a
kind of, not of the newest, Poor-John. A strange fish!
Were I in England now, as once I was, and had but this
fish painted, not a holiday fool there but would give a
piece of silver: there would this monster make a man;
30 any strange beast there makes a man: when they will not
give a doit to relieve a lame beggar, they will lay out ten
to see a dead Indian. Legg'd like a man! and his fins like
arms! Warm, o' my troth! I do now let loose my opinion,
hold it no longer, — this is no fish, but an islander, that

---

l. 9 *mow*: grin.
l. 18 *bear*: keep.
l. 21 *bombard*: leather jug.

l. 26 *Poor-John*: salted hake.
l. 31 *doit*: half-farthing.

hath lately suffer'd by a thunderbolt. [*Thunder*.] Alas, the storm is come again! my best way is to creep under his gaberdine; there is no other shelter hereabout: misery acquaints a man with strange bedfellows. I will here shroud till the dregs of the storm be past. [*Creeps under Caliban's cloak, so that his head is next to Caliban's legs.*] *Enter Stephano, singing; a bottle in his hand. He is the King's butler, also from the wreck.*

STEPHANO

40   I shall no more to sea, to sea,
           Here shall I die ashore, —
This is a very scurvy tune to sing at a man's funeral: well, here's my comfort.   [*Drinks.*

    The master, the swabber, the boatswain, and I,
       The gunner, and his mate,
   Loved Mall, Meg, and Marian, and Margery,
      But none of us cared for Kate;
      For she had a tongue with a tang,
      Would cry to a sailor, Go hang!
50   She loved not the savour of tar nor of pitch; ...
      Then, to sea, boys, and let her go hang!
This is a scurvy tune too: but here's my comfort.

                                   [*Drinks.*

CALIBAN

Do not torment me: — O!

STEPHANO

What's the matter? Have we devils here? Do you put tricks upon 's with salvages and men of Inde? ha! I have not scaped drowning, to be afeard now of your four legs; for it hath been said, 'As proper a man as ever went on four legs cannot make him give ground'; and it shall be said so again, while Stephano breathes at nostrils.

l. 37 *gaberdine*: cloak.   l. 55 *men of Inde*: Indians.
l. 55 *salvages*: savages.   l. 58 *four* (really, two!).

CALIBAN

60 The spirit torments me: — O!

STEPHANO

This is some monster of the isle with four legs, who hath got, as I take it, an ague. Where the devil should he learn our language? I will give him some relief, if it be but for that. If I can recover him, and keep him tame, and get to Naples with him, he's a present for any emperor that ever trod on neat's-leather.

CALIBAN

Do not torment me, prithee; I'll bring my wood home faster.

STEPHANO

He's in his fit now, and does not talk after the wisest.
70 He shall taste of my bottle: if he have never drunk wine afore, it will go near to remove his fit. If I can recover him, and keep him tame, I will not take too much for him; he shall pay for him that hath him, and that soundly.

CALIBAN

Thou dost me yet but little hurt; thou wilt anon, I know it by thy trembling: now Prosper works upon thee.

STEPHANO

Come on your ways; open your mouth; here is that which will give language to you, cat: open your mouth; this will shake your shaking, I can tell you, and that
80 soundly: you cannot tell who's your friend: open your chaps again.

TRINCULO

I should know that voice: it should be — but he is drown'd; and these are devils: — O, defend me!

---

l. 62 *ague*: fever.
l. 66 *neat's*: ox.

l. 76 *trembling* (Stephano is rather drunk).

44

STEPHANO

Four legs and two voices, — a most delicate monster!
His forward voice, now, is to speak well of his friend; his
backward voice is to utter foul speeches and to detract.
If all the wine in my bottle will recover him, I will help
his ague. — Come, — Amen! I will pour some in thy
other mouth.

TRINCULO

90 Stephano!

STEPHANO

Doth thy other mouth call me? — Mercy, mercy! This
is a devil, and no monster: I will leave him; I have no
long spoon.

TRINCULO

Stephano! — if thou be'st Stephano, touch me, and
speak to me; for I am Trinculo, — be not afeard, — thy
good friend, Trinculo.

STEPHANO

If thou be'st Trinculo, come forth: I'll pull thee by the
lesser legs: if any be Trinculo's legs, these are they.
[*Draws Trinculo out by the legs.*] — Thou art very
100 Trinculo indeed! How camest thou to be the siege of
this moon-calf? can he vent Trinculos?

TRINCULO

I took him to be kill'd with a thunder-stroke. — But art
thou not drown'd, Stephano? I hope, now, thou are not
drown'd. Is the storm overblown? I hid me under the
dead moon-calf's gaberdine for fear of the storm. And
art thou living, Stephano? O Stephano, two Neapoli-
tans scaped!

---

l. 84 *delicate*: ingenious.
l. 86 *detract*: run down.
l. 93 *long spoon* (for supping
with the devil. Old proverb).

l. 100 *siege*: droppings.
l. 101 *moon-calf*: freak.
l. 101 *vent*: drop.

45

STEPHANO

Prithee, do not turn me about; my stomach is not constant.

CALIBAN [*aside*]

110 These be fine things, an if they be not sprites.
That's a brave god, and bears celestial liquor:
I will kneel to him.

STEPHANO

How didst thou scape? How camest thou hither? swear, by this bottle, how thou camest hither. I escaped upon a butt of sack, which the sailors heaved overboard, by this bottle! which I made of the bark of a tree with mine own hands, since I was cast ashore.

CALIBAN

I'll swear, upon that bottle, to be thy true subject; for the liquor is not earthly.

STEPHANO

120 Here; swear, then, how thou escapedst.

TRINCULO

Swum ashore, man, like a duck: I can swim like a duck, I'll be sworn.

STEPHANO

Here, kiss the book. Though thou canst swim like a duck, thou art made like a goose.

TRINCULO

O Stephano, hast any more of this?

STEPHANO

The whole butt, man: my cellar is in a rock by the seaside, where my wine is hid. — How now, moon-calf! how does thine ague?

CALIBAN

Hast thou not dropp'd from heaven?

---

l. 115 *sack*: wine.

STEPHANO

130 Out o' the moon, I do assure thee: I was the man-i'-the moon when time was.

CALIBAN

I have seen thee in her, and I do adore thee: my mistress show'd me thee, and thy dog, and thy bush.

STEPHANO

Come, swear to that; kiss the book: — I will furnish it anon with new contents: — swear.

TRINCULO

By this good light, this is a very shallow monster! — I afeard of him! — a very weak monster: — the man-i'-the-moon! — a most poor credulous monster! — Well drawn, monster, in good sooth!

CALIBAN

140 I'll show thee every fertile inch o' the island; and I will kiss thy foot: I prithee, be my god.

TRINCULO

By this light, a most perfidious and drunken monster! when's god's asleep, he'll rob his bottle.

CALIBAN

I'll kiss thy foot; I'll swear myself thy subject.

STEPHANO

Come on, then; down, and swear.

TRINCULO

I shall laugh myself to death at this puppy-headed monster: a most scurvy monster! I could find in my heart to beat him, —

STEPHANO

Come kiss.

TRINCULO

150 But that the poor monster's in drink: an abominable monster!

l. 139 *drawn*: drained.

47

CALIBAN

I'll show thee the best springs; I'll pluck thee berries;
I'll fish for thee, and get thee wood enough.
A plague upon the tyrant that I serve!
I'll bear him no more sticks, but follow thee,
Thou wondrous man.

TRINCULO

A most ridiculous monster, to make a wonder of a poor
drunkard!

CALIBAN

I prithee, let me bring thee where crabs grow;
160 And I with my long nails will dig thee pig-nuts;
Show thee a jay's nest, and instruct thee how
To snare the nimble marmoset; I'll bring thee
To clustering filberts, and sometimes I'll get thee
Young seamells from the rock. Wilt thou go with me?

STEPHANO

I prithee now, lead the way, without any more talking. —
Trinculo, the king and all our company else being
drown'd, we will inherit here. Here, bear my bottle:
fellow Trinculo, we'll find him by and by again.

CALIBAN [*sings drunkenly*]

Farewell, master; farewell, farewell!

TRINCULO

170 A howling monster; a drunken monster!

CALIBAN

No more dams I'll make for fish;
    Nor fetch in firing
    At requiring;
Nor scrape trenchering, nor wash dish:
    'Ban, 'Ban, Ca-Caliban
Has a new master: get a new man.

---

l. 162 *marmoset*: monkey.   l. 164 *seamells*: sea-birds.
l. 163 *filberts*: nuts.   l. 174 *trenchering*: plates.

Freedom, high-day! high-day, freedom! freedom, high-day, freedom!

STEPHANO

O brave monster! lead the way.   [*Exeunt*.

2

Another part of the Island. Enter Caliban, Stephano, and Trinculo.

STEPHANO

TELL not me; when the butt is out, we will drink water; not a drop before: therefore bear up, and board 'em! Servant-monster, drink to me.

TRINCULO

Servant-monster! the folly of this island! They say there's but five upon this isle: we are three of them; if the other two be brain'd like us, the state totters.

STEPHANO

Drink, servant-monster, when I bid thee: thy eyes are almost set in thy head.

TRINCULO

Where should they be set else? he were a brave monster
10   indeed, if they were set in his tail.

STEPHANO

My man-monster hath drown'd his tongue in sack: for my part, the sea cannot drown me; I swam, ere I could recover the shore, five-and-thirty leagues — off and on — by this light. — Thou shalt be my lieutenant, monster, or my standard.

TRINCULO

Your lieutenant, if you list; he's no standard.

---

l. 6 *other two*: Prospero and Miranda.

l. 15 *standard*: standard-bearer.

l. 16 *list*: like.

49

STEPHANO

We'll not run, Monsieur Monster.

TRINCULO

Nor go neither: but you'll lie, like dogs; and yet say nothing neither.

STEPHANO

20 Moon-calf, speak once in thy life, if thou be'st a good moon-calf.

CALIBAN

How does thy honour? Let me lick thy shoe. I'll not serve him, he is not valiant.

TRINCULO

Thou liest, most ignorant monster: I am in case to justle a constable. Why, thou debosh'd fish, thou, was there ever man a coward that hath drunk so much sack as I to-day! Wilt thou tell a monstrous lie, being but half a fish and half a monster?

CALIBAN

Lo, how he mocks me! wilt thou let him, my lord?

TRINCULO

30 'Lord,' quoth he! — that a monster should be such a natural!

CALIBAN

Lo, lo, again! bite him to death, I prithee.

STEPHANO

Trinculo, keep a good tongue in your head: if you prove a mutineer, the next tree! The poor monster's my subject, and he shall not suffer indignity.

CALIBAN

I thank my noble lord. Wilt thou be pleased to hearken once again to the suit I made to thee?

---

l. 24 *in case to*: fit to.　　　l. 31 *natural*: booby.

STEPHANO

Marry, will I: kneel and repeat it; I will stand, and so
shall Trinculo.

Enter Ariel [invisible].

CALIBAN

40 As I told thee before, I am subject to a tyrant, — a
sorcerer, that by his cunning hath cheated me of the
island.

ARIEL [*imitating Trinculo's voice*]

Thou liest.

CALIBAN

Thou liest, thou jesting monkey, thou:
I would my valiant master would destroy thee!
I do not lie.

STEPHANO

Trinculo, if you trouble him any more in 's tale, by this
hand, I will supplant some of your teeth.

TRINCULO

Why, I said nothing.

STEPHANO

Mum, then, and no more. — Proceed.

CALIBAN

50 I say, by sorcery, he got this isle;
From me he got it. If thy greatness will,
Revenge it on him, for I know thou darest,
But this thing dare not, —

STEPHANO

That's most certain.

CALIBAN

Thou shalt be lord of it, and I'll serve thee.

STEPHANO

How now shall this be compass'd? Canst thou bring me
to the party?

---

l. 56 *compass'd*: arranged.

CALIBAN

Yea, yea, my lord: I'll yield him thee asleep,
Where thou mayst knock a nail into his head.

ARIEL

60 Thou liest; thou canst not.

CALIBAN

What a pied ninny's this! Thou scurvy patch!
I do beseech thy greatness, give him blows,
And take his bottle from him: when that's gone,
He shall drink naught but brine; for I'll not show him
Where the quick freshes are.

STEPHANO

Trinculo, run into no further danger: interrupt the
monster one word further, and, by this hand, I'll turn
my mercy out o' doors, and make a stockfish of thee.

TRINCULO

Why, what did I? I did nothing. I'll go further off.

STEPHANO

70 Didst thou not say he lied?

ARIEL

Thou liest.

STEPHANO

Do I so? take thou that! [*Strikes Trinculo*]. As you like
this, give me the lie another time.

TRINCULO

I did not give the lie. — Out o' your wits, and hearing
too? — A pox o' your bottle! this can sack and drinking
do — A murrain on your monster and the devil take
your fingers!

---

l. 61 *pied*: dressed-up.
l. 65 *freshes*: springs.
l. 68 *stockfish*: dried cod (beaten before cooked).

l. 73 *give me the lie*: call me liar.
l. 75 *A pox o'*: blast.
l. 76 *murrain*: curse.

CALIBAN

Ha, ha, ha!

STEPHANO

80 Now, forward with your tale. — Prithee, stand further off.

CALIBAN

Beat him enough: after a little time,
I'll beat him too.

STEPHANO

Stand further. — Come, proceed.

CALIBAN

Why, as I told thee, 'tis a custom with him
I' the afternoon to sleep: then thou mayst brain him,
Having first seiz'd his books; or with a log
Batter his skull, or paunch him with a stake,
Or cut his wesand with thy knife: remember,
First to possess his books; for without them
He's but a sot, as I am, nor hath not
90 One spirit to command: they all do hate him
As rootedly as I: — burn but his books.
He has brave utensils, — for so he calls them, —
Which, when he has a house, he'll deck withal:
And that most deeply to consider is
The beauty of his daughter; he himself
Calls her a nonpareil: I never saw a woman,
But only Sycorax my dam and she;
But she as far surpasseth Sycorax
As great'st does least.

STEPHANO

Is it so brave a lass?

CALIBAN

100 Ay, lord; she will become thy bed, I warrant.
And bring thee forth brave brood.

---

l. 87 *wesand*: wind-pipe.   l. 97 *dam*: mother.
l. 96 *a nonpareil*: incomparable.

STEPHANO

Monster, I will kill this man: his daughter and I will be king and queen, — save our graces! — and Trinculo and thyself shall be viceroys. — Dost thou like the plot, Trinculo?

TRINCULO

Excellent.

STEPHANO

Give me thy hand: I am sorry I beat thee, but, while thou livest, keep a good tongue in thy head.

CALIBAN

Within this half hour will he be asleep:
110 Wilt thou destroy him then?

STEPHANO

Ay, on mine honour.

ARIEL

This will I tell my master.

CALIBAN

Thou makest me merry; I am full of pleasure
Let us be jocund: will you troll the catch
You taught me but while-ere?

STEPHANO

At thy request, monster, I will do reason, any reason. —
Come on, Trinculo, let us sing.   [*Sings.*

Flout 'em and scout 'em, and scout 'em
and flout 'em;
Thought is free.

CALIBAN

That's not the tune.

[*Ariel plays a tune on a tabor and pipe.*

---

l. 113 *jocund*: jolly.
l. 113 *troll the catch*: sing the song.

l. 117 *Flout 'em and scout 'em*: Let's make fun of them.
l. 119 *tabor*: little drum.

STEPHANO

120 What is this same?

TRINCULO

This is the tune of our catch, played by the picture of
Nobody.

STEPHANO

It thou be'st a man, show thyself in thy likeness: if thou
be'st a devil, take't as thou list.

TRINCULO

O, forgive me my sins!

STEPHANO

He that dies pays all debts: I defy thee. — Mercy upon
us!

CALIBAN

Art thou afeard?

STEPHANO

No, monster, not I.

CALIBAN

130 Be not afeard; the isle is full of noises,
Sounds, and sweet airs, that give delight, and hurt not.
Sometimes a thousand twangling instruments
Will hum about mine ears; and sometime voices
That, if I then had wak'd after long sleep,
Will make me sleep again: and then, in dreaming,
The clouds methought would open, and show riches
Ready to drop upon me; that, when I wak'd,
I cried to dream again.

STEPHANO

This will prove a brave kingdom to me, where I shall
140 have my music for nothing.

CALIBAN

When Prospero is destroy'd.

STEPHANO

That shall be by and by: I remember the story.

TRINCULO

The sound is going away; let's follow it, and after do our work.

STEPHANO

Lead, monster; we'll follow. — I would I could see this taborer! he lays it on.

TRINCULO

Wilt come? I'll follow, Stephano.   [*Exeunt.*

3

Before Prospero's Cave. The enchanter has conjured up three goddesses to bless Miranda, his daughter, and Prince Ferdinand of Naples, who are to be married.

JUNO*

1   HONOUR, riches, marriage-blessing,
      Long continuance, and increasing,
      Hourly joys be still upon you!
      Juno sings her blessings on you.

CERES†

      Earth's increase, foison plenty,
      Barns and garners never empty;
      Vines with clustering bunches growing;
      Plants with goodly burden bowing, ...
      Scarcity and want shall shun you;

10   Ceres' blessing so is on you.

FERDINAND

      This is a most majestic vision, and
      Harmonious charmingly. May I be bold
      To think these spirits?

---

* Queen of the Gods.   l. 5 *foison*: harvest.
† Goddess of Plenty.

56

PROSPERO

                Spirits, which by mine art
I have from their confines call'd to enact
My present fancies.

FERDINAND

                Let me live here ever;
So rare a wonder'd father, and a wise,
Makes this place Paradise.

MIRANDA

                    Sweet, now, silence!
Juno and Ceres whisper seriously;
There's something else to do; hush, and be mute,
20 Or else our spell is marr'd.

IRIS*

You nymphs, call'd Naiads, of the windring brooks,
With your sedg'd crowns and ever-harmless looks,
Leave your crisp channels, and on this green land
Answer your summons; Juno does command:
Come, temperate nymphs, and help to celebrate
A contract of true love; be not too late.

                    [Enter certain Nymphs.

You sunburnt sicklemen, of August weary,
Come hither from the furrow, and be merry:
Make holiday; your rye-straw hats put on,
30 And these fresh nymphs encounter every one
In country footing.

*Enter certain Reapers, properly habited: they join with the
Nymphs in a graceful dance; towards the end whereof Prospero
starts suddenly, and speaks; after which, to a strange, hollow,
and confused noise, they vanish.*

---

* The Messenger-Goddess.
  l. 22 *sedg'd*: made of rushes.
l. 21 *windring*: winding or wandering.
  l. 25 *temperate*: gentle.
  l. 31 *footing*: dancing.

PROSPERO [*aside*]

I had forgot that foul conspiracy
Of the beast Caliban and his confederates
Against my life: the minute of their plot
Is almost come. — [*to the Spirits*] Well done; — avoid, —
    no more.

FERDINAND

This is strange: your father's in some passion
That works him strongly.

MIRANDA

                    Never till this day
Saw I him touch'd with anger so distemper'd.

PROSPERO

You do look, my son, in a moved sort,
40   As if you were dismay'd: be cheerful, sir.
Our revels now are ended. These our actors,
As I foretold you, were all spirits, and
Are melted into air, into thin air:
And, like the baseless fabric of this vision,
The cloud-capp'd towers, the gorgeous palaces,
The solemn temples, the great globe itself,
Yea, all which it inherit, shall dissolve,
And, like this insubstantial pageant faded,
Leave not a rack behind. We are such stuff
50   As dreams are made on; and our little life
Is rounded with a sleep. — Sir, I am vex'd;
Bear with my weakness; my old brain is troubled:
Be not disturb'd with my infirmity:
If you be pleas'd, retire into my cell,
And there repose: a turn or two I'll walk.
To still my beating mind.

FERDINAND *and* MIRANDA

                    We wish your peace. [*Exeunt.*

l. 49 *rack*: cloud.

PROSPER [*to Ariel*]

Come with a thought! — I think thee, Ariel, come!

Enter Ariel

ARIEL

Thy thoughts I cleave to. What's thy pleasure?

PROSPERO

Spirit,

We must prepare to meet with Caliban.

ARIEL

60 Ay, my commander: when I presented Ceres,
I thought to have told thee of it; but I fear'd
Lest I might anger thee.

PROSPERO

Say again, where didst thou leave these varlets?

ARIEL

I told you, sir, they were red-hot with drinking;
So full of valour that they smote the air
For breathing in their faces; beat the ground
For kissing of their feet; yet always bending
Towards their project. Then I beat my tabor;
At which, like unback'd colts, they prick'd their ears,
70 Advanc'd their eyelids, lifted up their noses
As they smelt music: so I charm'd their ears,
That, calf-like, they my lowing follow'd through
Tooth'd briers, sharp furzes, pricking goss, and thorns,
Which enter'd their frail shins: at last I left them
I' the filthy-mantled pool beyond your cell,
There dancing up to the chins, that the foul lake
O'erstunk their feet.

PROSPERO

This was well done, my bird.

Thy shape invisible retain thou still.

---

l. 60 *presented*: played the part of.   l. 75 *mantled*: covered.

The trumpery in my house, go bring it hither,
80 For stale to catch these thieves.

ARIEL

        I go, I go.   [*Exit.*

PROSPERO

A devil, a born devil, on whose nature
Nurture can never stick; on whom my pains,
Humanely taken, all, all lost, quite lost;
And as with age his body uglier grows,
So his mind cankers. I will plague them all,
Even to roaring.

        [*Enter Ariel, loaded with glistening apparel.*
        Come, hang them on this line.

Prospero and Ariel remain, invisible. Enter Caliban, Stephano,
and Trinculo, all wet.

CALIBAN

Pray you, tread softly, that the blind mole may not
Hear a foot fall: we now are near his cell.

STEPHANO

Monster, your fairy, which you say is a harmless fairy,
90 has done little better than play'd the Jack with us.

TRINCULO

Monster, I do smell all horse-piss; at which my nose is
in great indignation.

STEPHANO

So is mine. — Do you hear, monster? If I should take a
displeasure against you, look you, —

TRINCULO

Thou wert but a lost monster.

CALIBAN

Good my lord, give me thy favour still.
Be patient, for the prize I'll bring thee to

---

l. 79 *trumpery*: gaudy clothes.   l. 82 *nurture*: education.
l. 80 *stale*: bait.

Shall hoodwink this mischance: therefore speak softly; —
All 's hush'd as midnight yet.

TRINCULO

100 Ay, but to lose our bottles in the pool, — !

STEPHANO

There is not only disgrace and dishonour in that,
monster, but an infinite loss.

TRINCULO

That's more to me than my wetting: yet this is your
harmless fairy, monster.

STEPHANO

I will fetch off my bottle, though I be o'er ears for my
labour.

CALIBAN

Prithee, my king, be quiet. See'st thou here,
This is the mouth o' the cell: no noise, and enter.
Do that good mischief which may make this island
110 Thine own for ever, and I, thy Caliban,
For aye thy foot-licker.

STEPHANO

Give me thy hand. I do begin to have bloody thoughts.

TRINCULO

O King Stephano! O peer! O worthy Stephano! look
what a wardrobe here is for thee!

CALIBAN

Let it alone, thou fool; it is but trash.

TRINCULO

O, ho, monster! we know what belongs to a frippery. —
O King Stephano!

STEPHANO

Put off that gown, Trinculo: by this hand, I'll have that
gown.

---

l. 116 *belongs to a frippery*:
what gay clothes are for.

TRINCULO

120 Thy grace shall have it.

CALIBAN

The dropsy drown this fool! what do you mean
To dote thus on such luggage? Let's all on,
And do the murder first: if he awake,
From toe to crown he'll fill our skins with pinches;
Make us strange stuff.

STEPHANO

Be you quiet, monster. — Mistress line, is not this my
jerkin? ...

TRINCULO

We steal by line and level, an't like your grace.

STEPHANO

I thank thee for that jest; here's a garment for 't: wit
130 shall not go unrewarded while I am king of this country.
'Steal by line and level' is an excellent pass of pate;
there's another garment for 't.

TRINCULO

Monster, come, put some lime upon your fingers, and
away with the rest.

CALIBAN

I will have none on 't: we shall lose our time,
And all be turn'd to barnacles, or to apes
With foreheads villainous low.

STEPHANO

Monster, lay-to your fingers: help to bear this away
where my hogshead of wine is, or I'll turn you out of
140 my kingdom: go to, carry this.

TRINCULO

And this.

---

l. 128 *by line and level*: cleverly.   l. 133 *put some lime upon your*
l. 131 *pass of pate*: brain-wave.   *fingers* (to make them sticky).

STEPHANO

Ay, and this.

A noise of hunters heard. Enter divers Spirits, in the shape of
hounds, hunting them about; Prospero and Ariel setting them on.

PROSPERO

Hey, Mountain, hey!

ARIEL

Silver! there it goes, Silver!

PROSPERO

Fury, Fury! there, Tyrant, there! hark, hark!
　　　　[*Caliban, Stephano, and Trinculo are driven out.*
Go charge my goblins that they grind their joints
With dry convulsions; shorten up their sinews
With aged cramps; and more pinch-spotted make them
Than pard or cat-o'-mountain.

ARIEL

　　　　　　Hark, they roar!

PROSPERO

150 Let them be hunted soundly. At this hour
Lie at my mercy all mine enemies:
Shortly shall all my labours end, and thou
Shalt have the air at freedom: for a little
Follow, and do me service.

The Tempest, II. 2, III. 2, IV. 1

---

l. 143 *Mountain, Silver, Fury,*　　l. 149 *pard*: leopard.
Tyrant (hounds' names).

DETERMINED TO PROVE A VILLAIN

Richard, Duke of Gloucester, soon to get himself made King Richard III, is here shown as a black-hearted, hunch-backed villain, rejoicing in his villainy and taking a fiendish delight in the success of his audacious schemes. Not content with getting his brother Clarence gaoled for conspiracy against their elder brother, King Edward IV, Gloucester has the effrontery to make love to the Lady Anne Neville, whose father he has murdered and whose husband he has slain at Tewkesbury.

1

A Street in London. Enter Richard, Duke of Gloster.

1   Now is the winter of our discontent
Made glorious summer by this sun of York;
And all the clouds that lour'd upon our house
In the deep bosom of the ocean buried.
Now are our brows bound with victorious wreaths;
Our bruised arms hung up for monuments;
Our stern alarums chang'd to merry meetings,
Our dreadful marches to delightful measures.
Grim-visag'd war hath smooth'd his wrinkled front;
10   And now — instead of mounting barbed steeds
To fright the souls of fearful adversaries —
He capers nimbly in a lady's chamber
To the lascivious pleasing of a lute.
But I, that am not shap'd for sportive tricks,
Nor made to court an amorous looking-glass;
I, that am rudely stamp'd, and want love's majesty

---

l. 2 *sun of York* ('The Sun in Splendour' was the Yorkist emblem).

l. 10 *barbed*: armoured.

l. 13 *lascivious*: wanton.

To strut before a wanton ambling nymph;
I, that am curtail'd of this fair proportion,
Cheated of feature by dissembling nature,
20 Deform'd, unfinish'd, sent before my time
Into this breathing world, scarce half made up,
(And that so lamely and unfashionable
That dogs bark at me as I halt by them) —
Why, I, in this weak piping time of peace,
Have no delight to pass away the time,
Unless to spy my shadow in the sun,
And descant on mine own deformity:
And therefore, since I cannot prove a lover,
To entertain these fair well-spoken days,
30 I am determined to prove a villain,
And hate the idle pleasures of these days.
Plots have I laid, inductions dangerous,
By drunken prophecies, libels, and dreams,
To set my brother Clarence and the king
In deadly hate the one against the other:
And, if King Edward be as true and just
As I am subtle, false, and treacherous,
This day should Clarence closely be mew'd up,
About a prophecy, which says that 'G
40 Of Edward's heirs the murderer shall be'.
Dive, thoughts, down to my soul: — here Clarence
      comes.
            Enter Clarence, guarded, and Brakenbury.
Brother, good day: what means this armed guard
That waits upon your Grace?

---

l. 19 *feature*: shapeliness.

l. 19 *dissembling*: false.

l. 24 *piping* (because peaceful music – and not warlike – is now heard).

l. 27 *descant*: remark on.

l. 32 *inductions*: steps.

l. 36 *King Edward*: King Edward IV.

l. 39 *G* (his name was George).

CLARENCE

His majesty,
Tendering my person's safety, hath appointed
This conduct to convey me to the Tower.

GLOSTER

Upon what cause?

CLARENCE

Because my name is George.

GLOSTER

Alack, my lord, that fault is none of yours;
He should, for that, commit your godfathers: —
O, belike his majesty hath some intent
50 That you shall be new-christen'd in the Tower.
But what's the matter, Clarence? may I know?

CLARENCE

Yea, Richard, when I know; for I protest
As yet I do not: but, as I can learn,
He hearkens after prophecies and dreams;
And from the cross-row plucks the letter G,
And says a wizard told him that by G
His issue disinherited should be;
And, for my name of George begins with G,
It follows in his thought that I am he.
60 These, as I learn, and such-like toys as these,
Have mov'd his highness to commit me now.

GLOSTER

Why, this it is, when men are rul'd by women: —
'Tis not the king that sends you to the Tower;
My Lady Grey his wife, Clarence, 'tis she
That tempers him to this extremity.
Was it not she, and that good man of worship,
Anthony Woodville, her brother there,

---

l. 44 *tendering*: watching over. l. 61 *commit*: imprison.
l. 55 *cross-row*: alphabet. l. 65 *tempers*: influences.

That made him send Lord Hastings to the Tower,
From whence this present day he is deliver'd?
70 We are not safe, Clarence; we are not safe.

CLARENCE

By heaven, I think there's no man is secure
But the queen's kindred, and night-walking heralds
That trudge betwixt the king and Mistress Shore.
Heard ye not what an humble suppliant
Lord Hastings was to her for his delivery?

GLOSTER

Humbly complaining to her deity
Got my lord chamberlain his liberty.
I'll tell you what, — I think it is our way,
If we will keep in favour with the king,
80 To be her men, and wear her livery:
The jealous o'erworn widow and herself,
Since that our brother dubb'd them gentlewomen,
Are mighty gossips in this monarchy.

BRAKENBURY

I beseech your Graces both to pardon me;
His majesty hath straitly given in charge
That no man shall have private conference,
Of what degree soever, with his brother.

GLOSTER

Even so; an please your worship, Brakenbury,
You may partake of any thing we say:
90 We speak no treason, man; — we say the king
Is wise and virtuous; and his noble queen
Well struck in years, fair, and not jealous; —
We say that Shore's wife hath a pretty foot,
A cherry lip, a bonny eye, a passing pleasing tongue;

---

l. 73 *Mistress Shore*: the King's
mistress.

l. 81 *widow*: the Queen.
l. 83 *mighty gossips*: influential.

And that the queen's kindred are made gentlefolks:
How say you, sir? can you deny all this?

BRAKENBURY

With this, my lord, myself have naught to do ...
I beseech your Grace to pardon me; and, withal,
Forbear your conference with the noble duke.

CLARENCE

100 We know thy charge, Brakenbury, and will obey.

GLOSTER

We are the queen's abjects, and *must* obey. —
Brother, farewell: I will unto the king;
And whatsoe'er you will employ me in, ...
I will perform it to enfranchise you.
Meantime, this deep disgrace in brotherhood
Touches me deeper than you can imagine.

CLARENCE

I know it pleaseth neither of us well.

GLOSTER

Well, your imprisonment shall not be long;
I will deliver you, or else lie for you:
110 Meantime, have patience.

CLARENCE

              I must perforce: farewell.

[*Exeunt Clarence, Brakenbury, and Guard.*

GLOSTER

Go, tread the path that thou shalt ne'er return,
Simple, plain Clarence! — I do love thee so,
That I will shortly send thy soul to heaven,
If heaven will take the present at our hands. —
But who comes here? the new-deliver'd Hastings?

Enter Hastings.

---

l. 104 *enfranchise*: set you free.   l. 109 *lie for you*: go there instead.

HASTINGS

Good time of day unto my gracious lord!

GLOSTER

As much unto my good lord chamberlain!
Well are you welcome to the open air.
How hath your lordship brook'd imprisonment?

HASTINGS

120 With patience, noble lord, as prisoners must:
But I shall live, my lord, to give them thanks
That were the cause of my imprisonment.

GLOSTER

No doubt, no doubt; and so shall Clarence too;
For they that were your enemies are his,
And have prevail'd as much on him as you.

HASTINGS

More pity that the eagle should be mew'd,
While kites and buzzards prey at liberty.

GLOSTER

What news abroad?

HASTINGS

No news so bad abroad as this at home:
130 The king is sickly, weak, and melancholy,
And his physicians fear him mightily.

GLOSTER

Now, by Saint Paul, this news is bad indeed.
O, he hath kept an evil diet long,
And overmuch consum'd his royal person:
'Tis very grievous to be thought upon.
What, is he in his bed?

HASTINGS

He is.

GLOSTER

Go you before, and I will follow you.   [*Exit Hastings*.

l. 126 *mew'd*: caged.

He cannot live, I hope; and must not die
140 Till George be pack'd with post-horse up to heaven.
I'll in, to urge his hatred more to Clarence,
With lies well steel'd with weighty arguments;
And, if I fail not in my deep intent,
Clarence hath not another day to live:
Which done, God take King Edward to his mercy,
And leave the world for me to bustle in!
For then I'll marry Warwick's youngest daughter:
What though I kill'd her husband and her father?
The readiest way to make the wench amends
150 Is to become her husband and her father:
The which will I; not all so much for love
As for another secret close intent,
By marrying her which I must reach unto.
But yet I run before my horse to market:
Clarence still breathes; Edward still lives and reigns:
When they are gone, then must I count my gains.

2

Enter the corpse of King Henry the Sixth, with gentlemen-at-arms to guard it, Lady Anne being the mourner.

LADY ANNE

1 SET down, set down your honourable load, —
If honour may be shrouded in a hearse, —
Whilst I awhile obsequiously lament
Th' untimely fall of virtuous Lancaster.
Poor key-cold figure of a holy king!
Pale ashes of the house of Lancaster!
Thou bloodless remnant of that royal blood!
Be it lawful that I invocate thy ghost,

---

l. 3 *obsequiously*: dutifully.
l. 4 *Lancaster*: King Henry VI, her father-in-law.

l. 8 *invocate*: call.

To hear the lamentations of poor Anne,
10 Wife to thy Edward, to thy slaughter'd son,
Stabb'd by the selfsame hand that made these wounds!
Lo, in these windows that let forth thy life,
I pour the helpless balm of my poor eyes: —
O, cursed be the hand that made these holes!
Cursed the heart that had the heart to do it!
Cursed the blood that let this blood from hence!
More direful hap betide that hated wretch,
That makes us wretched by the death of thee,
Than I can wish to adders, spiders, toads,
20 Or any creeping venom'd thing that lives!
If ever he have child, abortive be it,
Prodigious, and untimely brought to light,
Whose ugly and unnatural aspect
May fright the hopeful mother at the view;
And that be heir to his unhappiness!
If ever he have wife, let her be made
More miserable by the death of him
Than I am made by my young lord and thee! —
Come now towards Chertsey with your holy load,
30 Taken from Paul's to be interred there;
And still, as you are weary of the weight,
Rest you, whiles I lament King Henry's corse.

Enter Gloster.

GLOSTER

Stay, you that bear the corse, and set it down.

LADY ANNE

What black magician conjures up this fiend,
To stop devoted charitable deeds?

---

l. 10 *slaughter'd* (at the Battle
of Tewkesbury).
l. 11 *hand* (Gloucester's).
l. 13 *balm*: tears.

l. 17 *betide*: befall.
l. 21 *abortive*: born too soon.
l. 22 *prodigious*: abnormal.

GLOSTER

Villains, set down the corse; or, by Saint Paul,
I'll make a corse of him that disobeys!

FIRST GENTLEMAN

My lord, stand back, and let the coffin pass.

GLOSTER

Unmanner'd dog! stand thou, when I command:
40 Advance thy halberd higher than my breast,
Or, by Saint Paul, I'll strike thee to my foot,
And spurn upon thee, beggar, for thy boldness.

LADY ANNE

What, do you tremble? are you all afraid?
Alas, I blame you not; for you are mortal,
And mortal eyes cannot endure the devil. —
Avaunt, thou dreadful minister of hell!
Thou hadst but power over his mortal body, —
His soul thou canst not have; therefore, be gone.

GLOSTER

Sweet saint, for charity, be not so curst.

LADY ANNE

50 Foul devil, for God's sake, hence, and trouble us not;
For thou hast made the happy earth thy hell,
Fill'd it with cursing cries and deep exclaims.
If thou delight to view thy heinous deeds,
Behold this pattern of thy butcheries.
O, gentlemen, see, see! dead Henry's wounds
Open their congeal'd mouths and bleed afresh!
Blush, blush, thou lump of foul deformity;
For 'tis thy presence that exhales this blood
From cold and empty veins, where no blood dwells;
60 Thy deed, inhuman and unnatural,
Provokes this deluge most unnatural. —

---

l. 53 *heinous*: hateful.   l. 56 *congeal'd*: clotted.

O God, which this blood mad'st, revenge his death!
O earth, which this blood drink'st, revenge his death!
Either heaven with lightning strike the murderer dead;
Or, earth, gape open wide, and eat him quick
As thou dost swallow up this good king's blood,
Which his hell-govern'd arm hath butchered!

GLOSTER

Lady, you know no rules of charity,
Which renders good for bad, blessings for curses.

LADY ANNE

70 Villain, thou know'st no law of God nor man:
No beast so fierce but knows some touch of pity.

GLOSTER

But I know none, and therefore am no beast.

LADY ANNE

O wonderful, when devils tell the truth!

GLOSTER

More wonderful, when angels are so angry. —
Vouchsafe, divine perfection of a woman,
Of these supposed evils, to give me leave,
By circumstance, but to acquit myself.

LADY ANNE

Vouchsafe, defus'd infection of a man,
For these known evils, but to give me leave,
80 By circumstance, to curse thy cursed self.

GLOSTER

Fairer than tongue can name thee, let me have
Some patient leisure to excuse myself.

LADY ANNE

Fouler than heart can think thee, thou canst make
No excuse current, but to hang thyself.

---

l. 77 *circumstance*: proofs.   l. 84 *current*: of any use.
l. 78 *defus'd infection*: you mis-
shapen disease!

GLOSTER

By such despair, I should accuse myself.

LADY ANNE

And, by despairing, shouldst thou stand excused
For doing worthy vengeance on thyself,
That didst unworthy slaughter upon others.

GLOSTER

Say that I slew them not?

LADY ANNE

Why, then, they are not dead:
90 But dead they are, and, devilish slave, by thee.

GLOSTER

I did not kill your husband.

LADY ANNE

Why, then, he is alive.

GLOSTER

Nay, he is dead; and slain by Edward's hand.

LADY ANNE

In thy foul throat thou liest: Queen Margaret saw
Thy murderous falchion smoking in his blood;
The which thou once didst bend against her breast,
But that thy brothers beat aside the point.

GLOSTER

I was provoked by her slanderous tongue,
That laid their guilt upon my guiltless shoulders.

LADY ANNE

Thou wast provoked by thy bloody mind,
100 That never dreamt on aught but butcheries:
Didst thou not kill this king?

GLOSTER

I grant ye.

---

l. 93 *Queen Margaret*: King   l. 94 *falchion*: sword.
Henry VI's Queen.

LADY ANNE

Dost grant me, hedgehog? then God grant me too
Thou mayst be damned for that wicked deed!
O, he was gentle, mild, and virtuous!

GLOSTER

The fitter for the King of heaven, that hath him.

LADY ANNE

He is in heaven, where thou shalt never come.

GLOSTER

Let him thank me, that holp to send him thither;
For he was fitter for that place than earth.

LADY ANNE

And thou unfit for any place but hell.

GLOSTER

110 Yes, one place else, if you will hear me name it.

LADY ANNE

Some dungeon.

GLOSTER

      Your bed-chamber.

LADY ANNE

Ill rest betide the chamber where thou liest!

GLOSTER

So will it, madam, till I lie with you.

LADY ANNE

I hope so.

GLOSTER

      I know so. But, gentle Lady Anne, —
To leave this keen encounter of our wits
And fall somewhat into a slower method, —
Is not the causer of the timeless deaths
Of these Plantagenets, Henry and Edward,
As blameful as the executioner?

LADY ANNE

120 Thou wast the cause and most accurs'd effect.

GLOSTER

Your beauty was the cause of that effect;
Your beauty, that did haunt me in my sleep
To undertake the death of all the world,
So I might live one hour in your sweet bosom.

LADY ANNE

If I thought that, I tell thee, homicide,
These nails should rend that beauty from my cheeks.

GLOSTER

These eyes could not endure that beauty's wrack;
You should not blemish it, if I stood by:
As all the world is cheered by the sun,
130 So I by that; it is my day, my life.

LADY ANNE

Black night o'ershade thy day, and death thy life!

GLOSTER

Curse not thyself, fair creature; thou art both.

LADY ANNE

I would I were, to be reveng'd on thee.

GLOSTER

It is a quarrel most unnatural
To be reveng'd on him that loveth thee.

LADY ANNE

It is a quarrel just and reasonable
To be reveng'd on him that kill'd my husband.

GLOSTER

He that bereft thee, lady, of thy husband
Did it to help thee to a better husband.

LADY ANNE

140 His better doth not breathe upon the earth.

GLOSTER

He lives that loves thee better than he could.

---

l. 127 *wrack*: wreck.

LADY ANNE

Name him.

GLOSTER

Plantagenet.

LADY ANNE

Why, that was he.

GLOSTER

The selfsame name, but one of better nature.

LADY ANNE

Where is he?

GLOSTER

Here. [*She spits at him.*] Why dost thou
spit at me?

LADY ANNE

Would it were mortal poison, for thy sake!

GLOSTER

Never came poison from so sweet a place.

LADY ANNE

Never hung poison on a fouler toad.
Out of my sight! thou dost infect mine eyes.

GLOSTER

Thine eyes, sweet lady, have infected mine.

LADY ANNE

150 Would they were basilisks, to strike thee dead!

GLOSTER

I would they were, that I might die at once;
For now they kill me with a living death.
Those eyes of thine from mine have drawn salt tears,
Sham'd their aspects with store of childish drops:
These eyes, which never shed remorseful tear,
No, when my father York and Edward wept
To hear the piteous moan that Rutland made

---

l. 150 *basilisks*: a legendary   its eyes.
reptile which could kill with

When black-fac'd Clifford shook his sword at him;
Nor when thy warlike father, like a child,
160 Told the sad story of my father's death,
And twenty times made pause to sob and weep,
That all the standers-by had wet their cheeks,
Like trees bedash'd with rain; in that sad time
My manly eyes did scorn an humble tear;
And what these sorrows could not thence exhale,
Thy beauty hath, and made them blind with weeping.
I never sued to friend nor enemy;
My tongue could never learn sweet smoothing words;
But, now thy beauty is propos'd my fee,
170 My proud heart sues, and prompts my tongue to speak.
                              [*She looks scornfully at him.*

Teach not thy lips such scorn; for they were made
For kissing, lady, not for such contempt.
If thy revengeful heart cannot forgive,
Lo, here I lend thee this sharp-pointed sword;
Which if thou please to hide in this true breast,
And let the soul forth that adoreth thee,
I lay it naked to the deadly stroke,
And humbly beg the death upon my knee.
                    [*He lays his breast open; she points at it with
                                                his sword.*

Nay, do not pause; for I did kill King Henry,
180 But 'twas thy beauty that provoked me.
Nay, now dispatch; 'twas I that stabb'd young Edward,
But 'twas thy heavenly face that set me on.
                              [*She lets fall the sword.*

Take up the sword again, or take up me.

---

l. 158 *shook his sword at him*
(Yorkist leaders had been
slaughtered at the Battle of
Wakefield).

l. 167 *sued to*: begged of.
l. 169 *propos'd my fee*: con-
sidered as my reward.

LADY ANNE

Arise, dissembler: though I wish thy death,
I will not be thy executioner.

GLOSTER

Then bid me kill myself, and I will do it.

LADY ANNE

I have already.

GLOSTER

    That was in thy rage:
Speak it again, and, even with the word,
This hand, which for thy love did kill thy love,
190 Shall for thy love kill a far truer love;
To both their deaths shalt thou be accessary.

LADY ANNE

I would I knew thy heart.

GLOSTER

'Tis figur'd in my tongue.

LADY ANNE

I fear me both are false.

GLOSTER

Then never man was true.

LADY ANNE

Well, well, put up your sword.

GLOSTER

Say, then, my peace is made.

LADY ANNE

That shalt thou know hereafter.

GLOSTER

But shall I live in hope?

LADY ANNE

200 All men, I hope, live so.

GLOSTER

Vouchsafe to wear this ring.

---

l. 184 *dissembler*: trickster. l. 191 *accessary*: a contributor.

LADY ANNE

To take is not to give.

GLOSTER

Look, how this ring encompasseth thy finger,
Even so thy breast encloseth my poor heart;
Wear both of them, for both of them are thine.
And if thy poor devoted servant may
But beg one favour at thy gracious hand,
Thou dost confirm his happiness for ever.

LADY ANNE

What is it?

GLOSTER

210 That it may please you leave these sad designs
To him that hath more cause to be a mourner,
And presently repair to Crosby-place;
Where — after I have solemnly interr'd
At Chertsey monastery this noble king,
And wet his grave with my repentant tears —
I will with all expedient duty see you:
For divers unknown reasons, I beseech you,
Grant me this boon.

LADY ANNE

With all my heart; and much it joys me too
220 To see you are become so penitent. —

GLOSTER

Bid me farewell.

LADY ANNE

                    'Tis more than you deserve;
But since you teach me how to flatter you,
Imagine I have said farewell already.

[*Exit Lady Anne.*

GLOSTER

Sirs, take up the corse.

GENTLEMEN
>Towards Chertsey, noble lord?

GLOSTER

No, to White-Friars; there attend my coming.

>*[Exeunt all except Gloster.*

Was ever woman in this humour woo'd?
Was ever woman in this humour won?
I'll have her; — but I will not keep her long.
What! I, that kill'd her husband and his father,
230 To take her in her heart's extremest hate;
With curses in her mouth, tears in her eyes,
The bleeding witness of her hatred by;
Having God, her conscience, and these bars against me,
And I no friends to back my suit withal
But the plain devil and dissembling looks,
And yet to win her, — all the world to nothing!
Ha!
Hath she forgot already that brave prince,
Edward, her lord, whom I, some three months since,
240 Stabb'd in my angry mood at Tewkesbury?
A sweeter and a lovelier gentleman
(Fram'd in the prodigality of nature,
Young, valiant, wise, and, no doubt, right royal)
The spacious world cannot again afford:
And will she yet abase her eyes on me,
That cropp'd the golden prime of this sweet prince,
And made her widow to a woful bed?
On me, whose all not equals Edward's moiety?
On me, that halt and am mis-shapen thus?
250 My dukedom to a beggarly denier,

---

l. 226 *humour*: mood.
l. 235 *dissembling*: deceitful.
l. 242 *fram'd in the prodigality of nature*: endowed with every good gift.

l. 248 *moiety*: half.
l. 250 *denier*: very small sum.

I do mistake my person all this while:
Upon my life, she finds (although I cannot)
Myself to be a marvellous proper man.
I'll be at charges for a looking-glass;
And entertain a score or two of tailors
To study fashions to adorn my body:
Since I am crept in favour with myself,
I will maintain it with some little cost.
But first I'll turn yon fellow in his grave;
260 And then return lamenting to my love. —
Shine out, fair sun, till I have bought a glass,
That I may see my shadow as I pass.

King Richard III, I. 1-2

DOOM OF A DICTATOR

*A group of conspirators has plotted the murder of Julius Cæsar.
Its leaders are Cassius, who is jealous of the dictator, and
Brutus, whose friendship for Cæsar has had to give way to his
hatred of absolute rule. It has been arranged that Metellus
Cimber shall plead for his banished brother, and that while the
conspirators cluster round Cæsar's chair as if in support of
Cimber, the first blow shall be struck by Casca.*

*In the Senate House at Rome. Cæsar is surrounded by Brutus,
Cassius, Casca, Decius, Metellus, Cinna, Publius, and other
senators.*

---

l. 254 *be at charges for*: buy.

DOOM OF A DICTATOR

CAESAR

1   Are we all ready? What is now amiss
That Cæsar and his senate must redress?

METELLUS

Most high, most mighty, and most puissant Cæsar,
Metellus Cimber throws before thy seat
An humble heart, —   *[Kneeling.*

CAESAR

              I must prevent thee, Cimber.
These couchings and these lowly courtesies
Might fire the blood of ordinary men,
And turn pre-ordinance and first decree
Into the law of children. Be not fond,
10   To think that Cæsar bears such rebel blood
That will be thaw'd from the true quality
With that which melteth fools; I mean, sweet words,
Low-crooked curt'sies, and base spaniel-fawning.
Thy brother by decree is banished.
If thou dost bend, and pray, and fawn for him,
I spurn thee like a cur out of my way.
Know, Cæsar doth not wrong; nor without cause
Will he be satisfied.

METELLUS

Is there no voice more worthy than my own,
20   To sound more sweetly in great Cæsar's ear
For the repealing of my banish'd brother?

BRUTUS

I kiss thy hand, but not in flattery, Cæsar;
Desiring thee that Publius Cimber may
Have an immediate freedom of repeal.

---

l. 2 *redress*: put right.
l. 3 *puissant*: powerful.
l. 8 *turn pre-ordinance and first decree into the law of children*: make them disregard the laws and behave like children.
l. 9 *fond*: foolish.
l. 21 *repealing*: recalling.

CAESAR

What, Brutus!

CASSIUS

Pardon, Cæsar; Cæsar, pardon:
As low as to thy foot doth Cassius fall,
To beg enfranchisement for Publius Cimber.

CAESAR

I could be well mov'd, if I were as you;
If I could pray to move, prayers would move me:
30 But I am constant as the northern star,
Of whose true-fix'd and resting quality
There is no fellow in the firmament.
The skies are painted with unnumber'd sparks;
They are all fire, and every one doth shine;
But there's but one in all doth hold his place:
So in the world, — 'tis furnish'd well with men,
And men are flesh and blood, and apprehensive;
Yet in the number I do know but one
That unassailable holds on his rank,
40 Unshak'd of motion: and that I am he,
Let me a little show it, even in this, —
That I was constant Cimber should be banish'd,
And constant do remain to keep him so.

CINNA

O Cæsar, —

CAESAR

Hence! wilt thou lift up Olympus?

DECIUS

Great Cæsar, —

CAESAR

Doth not Brutus bootless kneel?

---

l. 27 *enfranchisement*: recall.
l. 37 *apprehensive*: intelligent.

l. 44 *Olympus*: mountain of the Gods.
l. 45 *bootless*: uselessly.

CASCA

Speak, hands, for me!   [*They stab Cæsar.*

CAESAR

Et tu, Brute? — Then fall, Cæsar!   [*Dies.*

CINNA

Liberty! Freedom! Tyranny is dead! —
Run hence, proclaim, cry it about the streets.

CASSIUS

50 Some to the common pulpits, and cry out,
'Liberty, freedom, and enfranchisement!'

BRUTUS

People, and senators, be not affrighted;
Fly not; stand still: — ambition's debt is paid.

CASCA

Go to the pulpit, Brutus.

DECIUS

           And Cassius too.

BRUTUS

Where's Publius?

CINNA

Here, quite confounded with this mutiny.

METELLUS

Stand fast together, lest some friend of Cæsar's
Should chance —

BRUTUS

Talk not of standing. — Publius, good cheer!
60 There is no harm intended to your person,
Nor to no Roman else: so tell them, Publius.

---

l. 47 *Et tu, Brute?*: What, Brutus too?

l. 50 *common pulpits*: public platforms.

l. 51 *enfranchisement*: freedom.

l. 56 *confounded with*: astonished at.

l. 59 *talk not of standing*: no need to band together!

CASSIUS

And leave us, Publius; lest that the people,
Rushing on us, should do your age some mischief.

BRUTUS

Do so: — and let no man abide this deed
But we the doers.

Enter Trebonius.

CASSIUS

Where is Anthony?

TREBONIUS

    Fled to his house amazed:
Men, wives, and children stare, cry out, and run
As it were doomsday.

BRUTUS

    Fates, we will know your pleasures: —
That we shall die, we know; 'tis but the time,
70 And drawing days out, that men stand upon.

CASSIUS

Why, he that cuts off twenty years of life
Cuts off so many years of fearing death.

BRUTUS

Grant that, and then is death a benefit:
So are we Cæsar's friends, that have abridg'd
His time of fearing death. — Stoop, Romans, stoop,
And let us bathe our hands in Cæsar's blood
Up to the elbows, and besmear our swords:
Then walk we forth, even to the market-place,
And, waving our red weapons o'er our heads,
80 Let's all cry, 'Peace, freedom, and liberty!'

CASSIUS

Stoop, then, and wash. — How many ages hence
Shall this our lofty scene be acted over
In states unborn and accents yet unknown!

---

l. 70 *stand upon*: worry about.

BRUTUS

How many times shall Cæsar bleed in sport,
That now on Pompey's basis lies along
No worthier than the dust!

CASSIUS

               So oft as that shall be,
So often shall the knot of us be call'd
The men that gave their country liberty.

DECIUS

What, shall we forth?

CASSIUS

            Ay, every man away:
90 Brutus shall lead; and we will grace his heels
With the most boldest and best hearts of Rome.

BRUTUS

Soft! who comes here?

          Enter a Servant.

          A friend of Anthony's.

SERVANT

Thus, Brutus, did my master bid me kneel;
Thus did Mark Anthony bid me fall down;
And, being prostrate, thus he bade me say: —
Brutus is noble, wise, valiant, and honest;
Cæsar was mighty, bold, royal, and loving:
Say I love Brutus, and I honour him;
Say I fear'd Cæsar, honour'd him, and lov'd him.
100 If Brutus will vouchsafe that Anthony
May safely come to him, and be resolv'd
How Cæsar hath deserv'd to lie in death,
Mark Anthony shall not love Cæsar dead
So well as Brutus living; but will follow
The fortunes and affairs of noble Brutus

---

l. 85 *Pompey's basis*: at the
foot of Pompey's statue.

l. 100 *vouchsafe*: allow.
l. 101 *resolv'd*: told.

Thorough the hazards of this untrod state
With all true faith. So says my master Anthony.

BRUTUS

Thy master is a wise and valiant Roman;
I never thought him worse.
110 Tell him, so please him come unto this place,
He shall be satisfied; and, by my honour,
Depart untouch'd.

SERVANT

        I'll fetch him presently.   [*Exit.*

BRUTUS

I know that we shall have him well to friend.

CASSIUS

I wish we may: but yet have I a mind
That fears him much; and my misgiving still
Falls shrewdly to the purpose.

BRUTUS

But here comes Anthony.

Enter Anthony.

        Welcome, Mark Anthony.

ANTHONY

O mighty Cæsar! dost thou lie so low?
Are all thy conquests, glories, triumphs, spoils,
120 Shrunk to this little measure? Fare thee well. —
I know not, gentlemen, what you intend,
Who else must be let blood, who else is rank:
If I myself, there is no hour so fit
As Cæsar's death's hour: nor no instrument
Of half that worth as those your swords, made rich
With the most noble blood of all this world.

---

l. 106 *thorough*: through.   l. 115 *still falls shrewdly to the*
l. 112 *presently*: now.   *purpose*: always turns out right.
                               l. 122 *rank*: ill.

I do beseech ye, if you bear me hard,
Now, whilst your purpled hands do reek and smoke,
Fulfil your pleasure. Live a thousand years,
130 I shall not find myself so apt to die:
No place will please me so, no mean of death
As here by Cæsar, and by you cut off,
The choice and master spirits of this age.

BRUTUS

O Anthony, beg not your death of us.
Though now we must appear bloody and cruel,
As, by our hands and this our present act,
You see we do; yet see you but our hands,
And this the bleeding business they have done:
Our hearts you see not, — they are pitiful;
140 And pity to the general wrong of Rome —
(As fire drives out fire, so pity pity) —
Hath done this deed on Cæsar. For your part,
To you our swords have leaden points, Mark Anthony,
Our arms no strength of malice; and our hearts,
Of brothers' temper, do receive you in
With all kind love, good thoughts, and reverence.

CASSIUS

Your voice shall be as strong as any man's
In the disposing of new dignities.

BRUTUS

Only be patient till we have appeased
150 The multitude, beside themselves with fear,
And then we will deliver you the cause,
Why I, that did love Cæsar when I struck him,
Have thus proceeded.

ANTHONY

I doubt not of your wisdom.

---

l. 127 *bear me hard*: dislike me.   l. 131 *mean*: way.

Let each man render me his bloody hand:
First, Marcus Brutus, will I shake with you: —
Next, Caius Cassius, do I take your hand; —
Now, Decius Brutus, yours; — now yours, Metellus; —
Yours, Cinna; — and, my valiant Casca, yours; —
Though last, not least in love, yours, good Trebonius.
160 Gentlemen all, — alas, what shall I say?
My credit now stands on such slippery ground,
That one of two bad ways you must conceit me:
Either a coward or a flatterer.
That I did love thee, Cæsar, O, 'tis true:
If, then, thy spirit look upon us now,
Shall it not grieve thee dearer than thy death,
To see thy Anthony making his peace,
Shaking the bloody fingers of thy foes,
(Most noble!) in the presence of thy corse?
170 Had I as many eyes as thou hast wounds,
Weeping as fast as they stream forth thy blood,
It would become me better than to close
In terms of friendship with thine enemies.
Pardon me, Julius! — Here wast thou bay'd, brave hart;
Here didst thou fall; and here thy hunters stand,
Sign'd in thy spoil, and crimson'd in thy lethe. —
O world, thou wast the forest to this hart;
And this, indeed, O world, the heart of thee. —
How like a deer, strucken by many princes,
180 Dost thou here lie!

CASSIUS

Mark Anthony, —

ANTHONY
Pardon me, Caius Cassius:

---

l. 162 *conceit*: think of.
l. 174 *bay'd*: brought to bay.

l. 176 *Sign'd in thy spoil, and crimson'd in thy lethe*: Blooded after the kill.

The enemies of Cæsar shall say this;
Then, in a friend, it is cold modesty.

CASSIUS

I blame you not for praising Cæsar so;
But what compact mean you to have with us?
Will you be prick'd in number of our friends;
Or shall we on, and not depend on you?

ANTHONY

Therefore I took your hands; but was, indeed,
Sway'd from the point, by looking down on Cæsar.
190 Friends am I with you all, and love you all;
Upon this hope, that you shall give me reasons
Why and wherein Cæsar was dangerous.

BRUTUS

Or else were this a savage spectacle:
Our reasons are so full of good regard,
That were you, Anthony, the son of Cæsar,
You should be satisfied.

ANTHONY

        That's all I seek:
And am moreover suitor that I may
Produce his body to the market-place;
And in the pulpit, as becomes a friend,
200 Speak in the order of his funeral.

BRUTUS

You shall, Mark Anthony.

CASSIUS

        Brutus, a word with you.
[*Aside to Brutus*] You know not what you do: do not consent
That Anthony speak in his funeral:

---

l. 183 *cold modesty*: faint praise.   l. 186 *prick'd*: listed.

Know you how much the people may be mov'd
By that which he will utter?

BRUTUS [*Aside to Cassius*]

By your pardon; —
I will myself into the pulpit first,
And show the reason of our Cæsar's death:
What Anthony shall speak, I will protest
He speaks by leave and by permission;
210 And that we are contented Cæsar shall
Have all true rites and lawful ceremonies.
It shall advantage more than do us wrong.

CASSIUS [*Aside to Brutus*]

I know not what may fall; I like it not.

BRUTUS

Mark Anthony, here, take you Cæsar's body.
You shall not in your funeral speech blame us,
But speak all good you can devise of Cæsar;
And say you do 't by our permission;
Else shall you not have any hand at all
About his funeral: and you shall speak
220 In the same pulpit whereto I am going,
After my speech is ended.

ANTHONY

Be it so;
I do desire no more.

BRUTUS

Prepare the body, then, and follow us.

[*Exeunt all but Anthony.*

ANTHONY

O, pardon me, thou bleeding piece of earth,
That I am meek and gentle with these butchers!
Thou art the ruins of the noblest man
That ever lived in the tide of times.
Woe to the hands that shed this costly blood!

Over thy wounds now do I prophesy, —
230 Which, like dumb mouths, do ope their ruby lips,
To beg the voice and utterance of my tongue, —
A curse shall light upon the limbs of men;
Domestic fury and fierce civil strife
Shall cumber all the parts of Italy;
Blood and destruction shall be so in use,
And dreadful objects so familiar,
That mothers shall but smile when they behold
Their infants quarter'd with the hands of war;
All pity chok'd with custom of fell deeds:
240 And Cæsar's spirit, ranging for revenge,
With Ate by his side come hot from hell,
Shall in these confines with a monarch's voice
Cry 'Havoc', and let slip the dogs of war;
That this foul deed shall smell above the earth
With carrion men, groaning for burial.

Enter Octavius' Servant.

You serve Octavius Cæsar, do you not?

SERVANT

I do, Mark Anthony.

ANTHONY

Cæsar did write for him to come to Rome.

SERVANT

He did receive his letters, and is coming;
250 And bid me say to you by word of mouth —
O Cæsar! —   [*Seeing the body.*

ANTHONY

Thy heart is big, get thee apart and weep.
Passion, I see, is catching; for mine eyes,
Seeing those beads of sorrow stand in thine,
Begin to water. Is thy master coming?

l. 240 *ranging* (like a hound).   l. 241 *Ate*: Vengeance.

SERVANT

He lies to-night within seven leagues of Rome.

ANTHONY

Post back with speed, and tell him what hath chanc'd:
Here is a mourning Rome, a dangerous Rome,
No Rome of safety for Octavius yet;
260 Hie hence, and tell him so. Yet, stay awhile;
Thou shalt not back till I have borne this corse
Into the market-place: there shall I try,
In my oration, how the people take
The cruel issue of these bloody men;
According to the which, thou shalt discourse
To young Octavius of the state of things.

Julius Cæsar, III. 1

RIOT IN THE FORUM

*Mark Anthony is an opportunist, and has decided to join
Octavius, Cæsar's adopted heir, who is on his way to Rome to
put down the movement led by Cassius and Brutus which has
brought about the assassination of the dictator. Meanwhile he
has to preside at Cæsar's funeral ceremony in the principal
square of Rome, where he is surrounded by a mob, stirred up
by Brutus and his friends to curse the memory — and indeed
the very name — of Cæsar.*

*In the Forum at Rome. Enter Brutus and Cassius, and a throng
of Citizens.*

CITIZENS

1   WE will be satisfied; let us be satisfied!

---

l. 264 *issue*: action.   l. 1 *satisfied* (that Cæsar's assassination was justifiable).

BRUTUS

Then follow me, and give me audience, friends.
Cassius, go you into the other street,
And part the numbers.
Those that will hear me speak, let 'em stay here;
Those that will follow Cassius, go with him;
And public reasons shall be rendered
Of Cæsar's death.

FIRST CITIZEN

I will hear Brutus speak.

SECOND CITIZEN

I will hear Cassius; and compare their reasons,
10 When severally we hear them rendered.

[*Exit Cassius, with some of the Citizens.
Brutus goes to the speaker's platform.*

THIRD CITIZEN

The noble Brutus is ascended: silence!

BRUTUS

Be patient till the last.
Romans, countrymen, and lovers! hear me for my cause;
and be silent, that you may hear: believe me for mine
honour; and have respect to mine honour, that you may
believe: censure me in your wisdom; and awake your
senses, that you may the better judge. If there be any in
this assembly, any dear friend of Cæsar's, to him I say,
that Brutus' love to Cæsar was no less than his. If, then,
20 that friend demand why Brutus rose against Cæsar, this
is my answer, — Not that I loved Cæsar less, but that I
loved Rome more. Had you rather Cæsar were living,
and die all slaves, than that Cæsar were dead, to live all
free men? As Cæsar loved me, I weep for him; as he was
fortunate, I rejoice at it; as he was valiant, I honour him:

---

l. 10 *severally*: by each of them.　　l. 15 *to*: for.
l. 13 *lovers*: friends.　　l. 16 *censure*: judge.

but, as he was ambitious, I slew him. There is tears for
his love; joy for his fortune; honour for his valour; and
death for his ambition. Who is here so base that would
be a bondman? If any, speak; for him have I offended.
30 Who is here so rude that would not be a Roman? If any,
speak; for him have I offended. Who is here so vile that
will not love his country? If any, speak; for him have I
offended. I pause for a reply.

CITIZENS

None, Brutus, none.

BRUTUS

Then none have I offended. I have done no more to
Cæsar than you shall do to Brutus. The question of his
death is enroll'd in the Capitol; his glory not extenuated,
wherein he was worthy; nor his offences enforced, for
which he suffer'd death. Here comes his body, mourn'd
40 by Mark Anthony:

Enter Anthony with Cæsar's body.

who, though he had no hand in his death, shall receive
the benefit of his dying, a place in the commonwealth; as
which of you shall not? With this I depart, — that, as I
slew my best lover for the good of Rome, I have the
same dagger for myself, when it shall please my country
to need my death.

CITIZENS

Live, Brutus! live, live!

FIRST CITIZEN

Bring him with triumph home unto his house.

SECOND CITIZEN

Give him a statue with his ancestors.

THIRD CITIZEN

50 Let him be Cæsar.

---

l. 29 *bondman*: slave.   l. 37 *extenuated*: underrated.
l. 30 *rude*: uncivilized.   l. 38 *enforced*: stressed.

FOURTH CITIZEN

    Cæsar's better parts

Shall be crown'd in Brutus.

FIRST CITIZEN

We'll bring him to his house with shouts and clamours.

BRUTUS

My countrymen, —

SECOND CITIZEN

    Peace, silence! Brutus speaks.

FIRST CITIZEN

Peace, ho!

BRUTUS

Good countrymen, let me depart alone,
And, for my sake, stay here with Anthony:
Do grace to Cæsar's corpse, and grace his speech
Tending to Cæsar's glories; which Mark Anthony,
By our permission, is allow'd to make.
60 I do entreat you, not a man depart,
Save I alone, till Anthony have spoke.   [*Exit.*

FIRST CITIZEN

Stay, ho! and let us hear Mark Anthony.

THIRD CITIZEN

Let him go up into the public chair;
We'll hear him. — Noble Anthony, go up.

ANTHONY

For Brutus' sake, I am beholden to you.   [*Goes up.*

FOURTH CITIZEN

What does he say of Brutus?

THIRD CITIZEN

    He says, for Brutus' sake,

He finds himself beholding to us all.

FOURTH CITIZEN

'Twere best he speak no harm of Brutus here.

---

l. 65 *beholden*: indebted.

97

FIRST CITIZEN

This Cæsar was a tyrant.

THIRD CITIZEN

        Nay, that's certain:

70   We are blest that Rome is rid of him.

SECOND CITIZEN

Peace! let us hear what Anthony can say.

ANTHONY

You gentle Romans, —

CITIZENS

        Peace, ho! let us hear him.

ANTHONY

Friends, Romans, countrymen, lend me your ears;
I come to bury Cæsar, not to praise him.
The evil that men do lives after them;
The good is oft interred with their bones:
So let it be with Cæsar. The noble Brutus
Hath told you Cæsar was ambitious:
If it were so, it was a grievous fault;
80   And grievously hath Cæsar answer'd it.
Here, under leave of Brutus and the rest, —
For Brutus is an honourable man;
So are they all, all honourable men, —
Come I to speak in Cæsar's funeral.
He was my friend, faithful and just to me:
But Brutus says he was ambitious;
And Brutus is an honourable man.
He hath brought many captives home to Rome,
Whose ransoms did the general coffers fill:
90   Did this in Cæsar seem ambitious?
When that the poor have cried, Cæsar hath wept:
Ambition should be made of sterner stuff:
Yet Brutus says he was ambitious;
And Brutus is an honourable man.

You all did see that on the Lupercal
I thrice presented him a kingly crown,
Which he did thrice refuse: was this ambition?
Yet Brutus says he was ambitious;
And, sure, he is an honourable man.
100 I speak not to disprove what Brutus spoke,
But here I am to speak what I do know.
You all did love him once, — not without cause:
What cause withholds you, then, to mourn for him?
O judgement, thou art fled to brutish beasts,
And men have lost their reason! — Bear with me;
My heart is in the coffin there with Cæsar,
And I must pause till it come back to me.

FIRST CITIZEN

Methinks there is much reason in his sayings.

SECOND CITIZEN

If thou consider rightly of the matter,
110 Cæsar has had great wrong.

THIRD CITIZEN

                Has he, masters?
I fear there will a worse come in his place.

FOURTH CITIZEN

Mark'd ye his words? He would not take the crown;
Therefore 'tis certain he was not ambitious.

FIRST CITIZEN

If it be found so, some will dear abide it.

SECOND CITIZEN

Poor soul! his eyes are red as fire with weeping.

THIRD CITIZEN

There's not a nobler man in Rome than Anthony.

FOURTH CITIZEN

Now mark him, he begins again to speak.

---

l. 95 *Lupercal*: a public festival.

ANTHONY

But yesterday the word of Cæsar might
Have stood against the world: now lies he there,
120 And none so poor to do him reverence.
O masters, if I were dispos'd to stir
Your hearts and minds to mutiny and rage,
I should do Brutus wrong, and Cassius wrong,
Who, you all know, are honourable men:
I will not do them wrong; I rather choose
To wrong the dead, to wrong myself, and you,
Than I will wrong such honourable men.
But here's a parchment with the seal of Cæsar, —
I found it in his closet, — 'tis his will:
130 Let but the commons hear this testament, —
Which, pardon me, I do not mean to read, —
And they would go and kiss dead Cæsar's wounds,
And dip their napkins in his sacred blood;
Yea, beg a hair of him for memory,
And, dying, mention it within their wills,
Bequeathing it, as a rich legacy,
Unto their issue.

FOURTH CITIZEN

We'll hear the will: read it, Mark Anthony.

CITIZENS

The will, the will! we will hear Cæsar's will.

ANTHONY

140 Have patience, gentle friends, I must not read it;
It is not meet you know how Cæsar lov'd you.
You are not wood, you are not stones, but men;
And, being men, hearing the will of Cæsar,
It will inflame you, it will make you mad:

---

l. 120 *poor*: low in rank.   l. 133 *napkins*: handkerchiefs.
l. 129 *closet*: cabinet for papers.

'Tis good you know not that you are his heirs;
For, if you should, O, what would come of it!

FOURTH CITIZEN

Read the will: we'll hear it, Anthony;
You shall read us the will, — Cæsar's will.

ANTHONY

Will you be patient? will you stay awhile?
150 I have o'ershot myself to tell you of it:
I fear I wrong the honourable men
Whose daggers have stabb'd Cæsar; I do fear it.

FOURTH CITIZEN

They were traitors: honourable men!

CITIZENS

The will! The testament!

SECOND CITIZEN

They were villains, murderers: the will! read the will.

ANTHONY

You will compel me, then, to read the will?
Then make a ring about the corpse of Cæsar,
And let me show you him that made the will.
Shall I descend? and will you give me leave?

CITIZENS

160 Come down.

SECOND CITIZEN

Descend.

THIRD CITIZEN

You shall have leave.

[*Anthony comes down.*

FOURTH CITIZEN

A ring; stand round.

FIRST CITIZEN

Stand from the hearse, stand from the body.

SECOND CITIZEN

Room for Anthony, — most noble Anthony.

ANTHONY

Nay, press not so upon me; stand far off.

CITIZENS

Stand back; room; bear back.

ANTHONY

If you have tears, prepare to shed them now.
You all do know this mantle: I remember
170 The first time ever Cæsar put it on;
'Twas on a summer's evening, in his tent,
That day he overcame the Nervii: —
Look, in this place ran Cassius' dagger through:
See what a rent the envious Casca made:
Through this the well-beloved Brutus stabb'd,
And, as he pluck'd his cursed steel away,
Mark how the blood of Cæsar follow'd it,
As rushing out of doors, to be resolved
If Brutus so unkindly knock'd, or no;
180 For Brutus, as you know, was Cæsar's angel:
Judge, O you gods, how dearly Cæsar lov'd him!
This was the most unkindest cut of all;
For when the noble Cæsar saw him stab,
Ingratitude, more strong than traitors' arms,
Quite vanquish'd him: then burst his mighty heart;
And, in his mantle muffling up his face,
Even at the base of Pompey's statua,
Which all the while ran blood, great Cæsar fell.
O, what a fall was there, my countrymen!
190 Then I, and you, and all of us fell down,
Whilst bloody treason flourish'd over us.
O, now you weep; and, I perceive, you feel
The dint of pity: these are gracious drops.
Kind souls, what, weep you when you but behold

---

l. 172 *Nervii*: a Belgic tribe.   l. 193 *dint*: force.
l. 180 *angel*: favourite.

Our Cæsar's vesture wounded? Look you here,
Here is himself, marr'd, as you see, with traitors.

FIRST CITIZEN

O piteous spectacle!

SECOND CITIZEN

O noble Cæsar!

THIRD CITIZEN

O woeful day!

FOURTH CITIZEN

200 O traitors, villains!

FIRST CITIZEN

O most bloody sight!

SECOND CITIZEN

We will be revenged.

CITIZENS

Revenge, — about, — seek, — burn, — fire, — kill, — slay,
— let not a traitor live!

ANTHONY

Stay, countrymen.

FIRST CITIZEN

Peace there! hear the noble Anthony.

SECOND CITIZEN

We'll hear him, we'll follow him, we'll die with him.

ANTHONY

Good friends, sweet friends, let me not stir you up
To such a sudden flood of mutiny.
210 They that have done this deed are honourable; —
What private griefs they have, alas, I know not,
That made them do it; — they are wise and honourable,
And will, no doubt, with reasons answer you.
I come not, friends, to steal away your hearts:
I am no orator, as Brutus is;
But, as you know me all, a plain blunt man,
That love my friend; and that they know full well

That gave me public leave to speak of him:
For I have neither wit, nor words, nor worth,
220 Action, nor utterance, nor the power of speech
To stir men's blood: I only speak right on;
I tell you that which you yourselves do know;
Show you sweet Cæsar's wounds — poor, poor dumb
And bid them speak for me: but were I Brutus, [mouths —
And Brutus Anthony, there were an Anthony
Would ruffle up your spirits, and put a tongue
In every wound of Cæsar, that should move
The stones of Rome to rise and mutiny.

CITIZENS

We'll mutiny.

FIRST CITIZEN

230 We'll burn the house of Brutus.

THIRD CITIZEN

Away, then! come, seek the conspirators.

ANTHONY

Yet hear me, countrymen; yet hear me speak.

CITIZENS

Peace, ho! hear Anthony, — most noble Anthony.

ANTHONY

Why, friends, you go to do you know not what.
Wherein hath Cæsar thus deserv'd your loves?
Alas, you know not, — I must tell you, then: —
You have forgot the will I told you of.

CITIZENS

Most true; the will: — let's stay and hear the will.

ANTHONY

Here is the will, and under Cæsar's seal: —
240 To every Roman citizen he gives,
To every several man, seventy-five drachmas.

l. 241 *seventy-five drachmas:*
£3 (1949).

SECOND CITIZEN

Most noble Cæsar! — we'll revenge his death.

THIRD CITIZEN

O royal Cæsar!

ANTHONY

Hear me with patience.

CITIZENS

Peace, ho!

ANTHONY

Moreover, he hath left you all his walks,
His private arbours, and new-planted orchards,
On this side Tiber; he hath left them you,
And to your heirs for ever, — common pleasures,
250 To walk abroad, and recreate yourselves.
Here was a Cæsar! when comes such another?

FIRST CITIZEN

Never, never. — Come, away, away!
We'll burn his body in the holy place,
And with the brands fire the traitors' houses.
Take up the body.

SECOND CITIZEN

Go fetch fire.

THIRD CITIZEN

Pluck down benches.

FOURTH CITIZEN

Pluck down forms, windows, any thing.

[Exeunt Citizens with the body.

ANTHONY

Now let it work: — mischief, thou art afoot,
260 Take thou what course thou wilt!

Enter Servant.

How now, fellow!

SERVANT

Sir, Octavius is already come to Rome.

ANTHONY

Where is he?

SERVANT

He and Lepidus are at Cæsar's house.

ANTHONY

And thither will I straight to visit him:
He comes upon a wish. Fortune is merry,
And in this mood will give us any thing.

SERVANT

I heard him say, Brutus and Cassius
Are rid like madmen through the gates of Rome.

ANTHONY

Belike they had some notice of the people
270 How I had mov'd them. Bring me to Octavius.

Julius Cæsar, III. 2

FALSTAFF IN GLOUCESTERSHIRE

*Sir John Falstaff — and who can help liking the fat rascal? —
because of his friendship with the Prince of Wales has been
commissioned to sign on men for the royal army which is to
oppose the rebels. Here he enjoys the hospitality of the ridiculous
country J.P., Shallow, and makes the acquaintance of his dim
cousin, Silence: he thinks that he may be able to turn this
acquaintanceship to some profit over and beyond the funny
stories he will be able to tell in London.*

1

*The Courtyard of Mr. Justice Shallow's House in Gloucester-
shire. Enter Shallow and Silence; Mouldy, Shadow, Wart,
Feeble, Bullcalf, and Servants, behind.*

106

SHALLOW

1 COME on, come on, come on, sir; give me your hand, sir,
give me your hand, sir: an early stirrer, by the rood!
And how doth my good cousin Silence?

SILENCE

Good morrow, good cousin Shallow.

SHALLOW

And how doth my good cousin, your bedfellow? and
your fairest daughter and mine, my god-daughter
Ellen?

SILENCE

Alas, a black ousel, cousin Shallow!

SHALLOW

By yea and nay, sir, I dare say my cousin William is
10 become a good scholar: he is at Oxford still, is he not?

SILENCE

Indeed, sir, to my cost.

SHALLOW

A' must, then, to the Inns o' Court shortly: I was once of
Clement's-inn, where I think they will talk of mad
Shallow yet.

SILENCE

You were call'd 'lusty Shallow' then, cousin.

SHALLOW

By the mass, I was call'd any thing; and I would have
done any thing indeed too, and roundly too. There was
I, and little John Doit of Staffordshire, and black George
Barnes, and Francis Pickbone, and Will Squele, a Cotsall
20 man, — you had not four such swinge-bucklers in all

---

l. 2 *rood*: Cross.
l. 8 *a black ousel*: black-haired.
('gentlemen preferred blondes')
l. 12 *to the Inns o' Court* (in
London, to study law).

l. 19 *Cotsall*: Cotswold.
l. 20 *swinge-bucklers*: dashing
fellows.

the inns o' court again: and, I may say to you, we knew
where the bona-robas were, and had the best of them all
at commandment. Then was Jack Falstaff, now Sir
John, a boy, and page to Thomas Mowbray, duke of
Norfolk.

SILENCE

This Sir John, cousin, that comes hither anon about
soldiers?

SHALLOW

The same Sir John, the very same. I see him break
Scoggin's head at the court-gate, when a' was a crack,
30 not thus high: and the very same day did I fight with one
Sampson Stockfish, a fruiterer, behind Gray's-inn. Jesu,
Jesu, the mad days that I have spent! and to see how
many of my old acquaintance are dead!

SILENCE

We shall all follow, cousin.

SHALLOW

Certain, 'tis certain; very sure, very sure: death, as the
Psalmist says, is certain to all; all shall die. — How a
good yoke of bullocks at Stamford fair?

SILENCE

Truly, cousin, I was not there.

SHALLOW

Death is certain. — Is old Double of your town living
40 yet?

SILENCE

Dead, sir.

SHALLOW

Jesu, Jesu, dead! — a' drew a good bow; — and dead! —
a' shot a fine shoot: — John o' Gaunt loved him well, and
betted much money on his head. Dead! — a' would have

---

l. 22 *bona-robas*: women.   l. 36 *how*: how much?

clapp'd i' th' clout at twelve score; and carried you a forehand shaft a fourteen and fourteen and a half, that it would have done a man's heart good to see. — How a score of ewes now?

SILENCE

Thereafter as they be: a score of *good* ewes may be worth
50 ten pounds.

SHALLOW

And is old Double dead?

SILENCE

Here come two of Sir John Falstaff's men, as I think.
Enter Bardolph.

BARDOLPH

Good morrow, honest gentlemen: I beseech you, which is Justice Shallow?

SHALLOW

I am Robert Shallow, sir; a poor esquire of this county, and one of the king's justices of the peace: what is your good pleasure with me?

BARDOLPH

My captain, sir, commends him to you; my captain, Sir John Falstaff, — a tall gentleman, by heaven, and a most
60 gallant leader.

SHALLOW

He greets me well, sir. I knew him a good backsword man. How doth the good knight? may I ask how my lady his wife doth?

BARDOLPH

Sir, pardon; a soldier is better accommodated than with a wife.

---

l. 45 *clapp'd i' th' clout at twelve score*: hit the target at 240 yds.
l. 46 *forehand shaft* (designed for short-range work).

l. 49 *thereafter as they be*: according to condition.
l. 61 *backsword man*: fencer at single-stick.

SHALLOW

It is well said, in faith, sir; and it is well said indeed too.
Better accommodated! — it is good; yea, indeed, is it:
good phrases are surely, and ever were, very commend-
able. Accommodated! — it comes of *accommodo*: very
70 good; a good phrase.

BARDOLPH

Pardon, sir; I have heard the word. Phrase call you it?
by this good day, I know not the phrase; but I will maintain the word with my sword to be a soldier-like word,
and a word of exceeding good command, by heaven.
Accommodated! that is, when a man is, as they say,
accommodated; or when a man is, being, whereby a'
may be thought to be accommodated; which is an excellent thing.

SHALLOW

It is very just. — Look, here comes good Sir John.
Enter Falstaff.
80 Give me your good hand, give me your worship's good
hand: by my troth, you like well, and bear your years
very well: welcome, good Sir John.

FALSTAFF

I am glad to see you well, good Master Robert Shallow: —
Master Surecard, as I think?

SHALLOW

No, Sir John; it is my cousin Silence, in commission
with me.

FALSTAFF

Good Master Silence, it well befits *you* should be of the
peace.

SILENCE

Your good worship is welcome.

---

l. 84 *Surecard*: 'dead cert'.   l. 85 *in commission*: a J.P.

FALSTAFF

90 Fie! this is hot weather, gentlemen. Have you provided
me here half a dozen sufficient men?

SHALLOW

Marry, have we, sir. Will you sit?

FALSTAFF

Let me see them, I beseech you.

SHALLOW

Where's the roll? where's the roll? where's the roll? —
Let me see, let me see, let me see. So, so, so, so, so, so,
so: yea, marry, sir: — Ralph Mouldy! — let them appear
as I call; let them do so, let them do so. — Let me see;
where is Mouldy?

MOULDY

Here, an't please you.

SHALLOW

100 What think you, Sir John? a good-limb'd fellow; young,
strong, and of good friends.

FALSTAFF

Is thy name Mouldy?

MOULDY

Yea, an't please you.

FALSTAFF

'Tis the more time thou wert used.

SHALLOW

Ha, ha, ha! most excellent, i' faith! things that are mouldy
lack use: very singular good! — in faith, well said, Sir
John; very well said.

FALSTAFF [to Shallow]

Prick him.

MOULDY

I was prick'd well enough before, an you could have let

---

l. 108 *prick him*: mark his
name.

l. 109 *prick'd*: worried (by being rounded up).

110 me alone: my old dame will be undone now, for one to
do her husbandry and her drudgery: you need not to
have prick'd me; there are other men fitter to go out
than I.

FALSTAFF

Go to: peace, Mouldy; you shall go. Mouldy, it is time
you were spent.

MOULDY

Spent!

SHALLOW

Peace, fellow, peace; stand aside: know you where you
are? — For th' other, Sir John: — let me see; — Simon
Shadow!

FALSTAFF

120 Yea, marry, let me have him to sit under: he's like to be
a cold soldier.

SHALLOW

Where's Shadow?

SHADOW

Here, sir.

FALSTAFF

Shadow, whose son art thou?

SHADOW

My mother's son, sir ...

SHALLOW

Do you like him, Sir John?

FALSTAFF

Shadow will serve for summer, — prick him ...

SHALLOW

Thomas Wart!

FALSTAFF

Where's he?

---

l. 116 *spent*: killed!   l. 121 *cold*: cool.

WART

130 Here, sir.

FALSTAFF

Is thy name Wart?

WART

Yea, sir.

FALSTAFF

Thou art a very ragged wart.

SHALLOW

Shall I prick him, Sir John?

FALSTAFF

It were superfluous; for his apparel is built upon his back, and the whole frame stands upon pins: prick him no more.

SHALLOW

Ha, ha, ha! — you can do it, sir; you can do it: I commend you well. — Francis Feeble!

FEEBLE

140 Here, sir.

FALSTAFF

What trade art thou, Feeble?

FEEBLE

A woman's tailor, sir.

SHALLOW

Shall I prick him, sir?

FALSTAFF

You may: but if he had been a man's tailor, he'ld ha' prick'd you. — Wilt thou make as many holes in an enemy's battle as thou hast done in a woman's petticoat?

FEEBLE

I will do my good will, sir; you can have no more.

FALSTAFF

Well said, good woman's tailor! well said, courageous Feeble! thou wilt be as valiant as the wrathful dove or

150 most magnanimous mouse. — Prick the woman's tailor
well, Master Shallow; deep, Master Shallow.

FEEBLE

I would Wart might have gone, sir.

FALSTAFF

I would thou wert a man's tailor, that thou mightst
mend him, and make him fit to go. I cannot put him to
a private soldier, that is the leader of so many thousands:
let that suffice, most forcible Feeble.

FEEBLE

It shall suffice, sir.

FALSTAFF

I am bound to thee, reverend Feeble. — Who is next?

SHALLOW

Peter Bullcalf o' th' green!

FALSTAFF

160 Yea, marry, let's see Bullcalf.

BULLCALF

Here, sir.

FALSTAFF

'Fore God, a likely fellow! — Come, prick me Bullcalf
till he roar again.

BULLCALF

Lord! good my lord captain, —

FALSTAFF

What, dost thou roar before thou art prick'd?

BULLCALF

O Lord, sir! I am a diseased man.

FALSTAFF

What disease hast thou?

BULLCALF

A cold, sir, — a cough, sir, — which I caught with

---

l. 155 *thousands*: of lice (in his
clothes).

ringing in the king's affairs upon his coronation-
170 day, sir.

FALSTAFF

Come, thou shalt go to the wars in a gown; we will have
away thy cold; and I will take such order, that thy friends
shall ring for thee. — Is here all?

SHALLOW

Here is two more call'd than your number; you must
have but four here, sir: — and so, I pray you, go in with
me to dinner.

FALSTAFF

Come, I will go drink with you, but I cannot tarry
dinner. I am glad to see you, by my troth, Master
Shallow.

SHALLOW

180 O, Sir John, do you remember since we lay all night in
the windmill in Saint George's field?

FALSTAFF

No more of that, good Master Shallow, no more of that.

SHALLOW

Ha, 'twas a merry night. And is Jane Nightwork alive?

FALSTAFF

She lives, Master Shallow.

SHALLOW

She never could away with me.

FALSTAFF

Never, never; she would always say she could not abide
Master Shallow.

SHALLOW

By the mass, I could anger her to the heart. She was
then a bona-roba. Doth she hold her own well?

---

l. 171 *gown*: night-gown.　　　　l. 173 *for thee*: for thy funeral.

FALSTAFF

190 Old, old, Master Shallow.

SHALLOW

Nay, she must be old; she cannot choose but be old; certain she's old; and had Robin Nightwork by old Nightwork before I came to Clement's-inn.

SILENCE

That's fifty-five year ago.

SHALLOW

Ha, cousin Silence, that thou hadst seen that that this knight and I have seen! — Ha, Sir John, said I well?

FALSTAFF

We have heard the chimes at midnight, Master Shallow.

SHALLOW

That we have, that we have, that we have; in faith, Sir John, we have: our watch-word was, 'Hem, boys!' — 200 Come, let's to dinner; come, let's to dinner: — Jesus, the days that we have seen! — come, come.

[*Exeunt Falstaff, Shallow, and Silence.*

BULLCALF

Good master corporate Bardolph, stand my friend; and here's four Harry ten shillings in French crowns for you. In very truth, sir, I had as lief be hang'd, sir, as go: and yet, for mine own part, sir, I do not care; but rather, because I am unwilling, and, for mine own part, have a desire to stay with my friends; else, sir, I did not care, for mine own part, so much.

BARDOLPH

Go to; stand aside.

MOULDY

210 And, good master corporal captain, for my old dame's sake, stand my friend: she has nobody to do any thing

---

l. 189 *bona-roba*: woman of the town.

l. 199 *Hem*: drink up!

l. 209 *go to*: get on with you!

about her when I am gone; and she is old, and cannot help herself: you shall have forty, sir.

BARDOLPH

Go to; stand aside.

FEEBLE

By my troth, I care not; a man can die but once; — we owe God a death: I'll ne'er bear a base mind: an't be my destiny, so; an't be not, so: no man's too good to serve 's prince; and let it go which way it will, he that dies this year is quit for the next.

BARDOLPH

220 Well said; thou'rt a good fellow.

FEEBLE

Faith, I'll bear no base mind.
Enter Falstaff, Shallow, and Silence.

FALSTAFF

Come, sir, which men shall I have?

SHALLOW

Four of which you please.

BARDOLPH [*Aside to Falstaff*]

Sir, a word with you: — I have three pound to free Mouldy and Bullcalf.

FALSTAFF

Go to; well!

SHALLOW

Come, Sir John, which four will you have?

FALSTAFF

Do you choose for me.

SHALLOW

Marry, then, — Mouldy, Bullcalf, Feeble, and Shadow.

FALSTAFF

230 Mouldy and Bullcalf: — for you, Mouldy, stay at home

---

l. 226 *go to*; *well*: that's good.

till you are past service: — and for your part, Bullcalf,
grow till you come unto it: — I will none of you.

SHALLOW

Sir John, Sir John, do not yourself wrong: they are your
likeliest men, and I would have you served with the best.

FALSTAFF

Will you tell me, Master Shallow, how to choose a man?
Care I for the limb, the thews, the stature, bulk, and big
assemblance of a man! Give me the spirit, Master Shallow. — Here's Wart; — you see what a ragged appearance
it is: a' shall charge you, and discharge you, with the
240 motion of a pewterer's hammer; come off, and on, swifter
than he that gibbets-on the brewer's bucket. And this
same half-faced fellow, Shadow, — give me this man:
he presents no mark to the enemy, — the foeman may
with as great aim level at the edge of a penknife. And,
for a retreat, — how swiftly will this Feeble, the woman's
tailor, run off! O, give me the spare men, and spare me
the great ones. — Put me a caliver into Wart's hand,
Bardolph.

BARDOLPH

Hold, Wart, traverse; thus, thus, thus.

FALSTAFF

250 Come, manage me your caliver. So: — very well — go
to: — very good: — exceeding good: — O, give me always
a little, lean, old, chapp'd, bald shot. — Well said, i' faith,
Wart: thou'rt a good scab: hold, there's a tester for thee.

SHALLOW

He is not his craft's-master; he doth not do it right. I

---

l. 239 *charge you*: load.
l. 239 *discharge you*: fire.
l. 241 *gibbets-on*: hoists.
l. 241 *bucket*: crane.
l. 247 *caliver*: gun.

l. 249 *traverse*: three paces
forward (?).
l. 252 *shot*: marksman.
l. 253 *tester*: sixpence.

remember at Mile-end Green, — when I lay at Clement's-inn, — I was then Sir Dagonet in Arthur's show, — there was a little quiver fellow, and a' would manage you his piece thus; and a' would about and about, and come you in and come you in: 'rah, tah, tah,' would a' say; 'bounce' would a' say; and away again would a' go, and again would a' come: — I shall ne'er see such a fellow.

FALSTAFF

These fellows will do well, Master Shallow. — God keep you, Master Silence: I will not use many words with you. — Fare you well, gentlemen both: I thank you: I must a dozen mile to-night. — Bardolph, give the soldiers coats.

SHALLOW

Sir John, the Lord bless you! God prosper your affairs! God send us peace! As you return, visit our house; let our old acquaintance be renew'd: peradventure I will with ye to the court.

FALSTAFF

'Fore God, I would you would, Master Shallow.

SHALLOW

Go to; I have spoke at a word; God keep you.

FALSTAFF

Fare you well, gentle gentlemen. [*Exeunt Shallow and Silence.*] On, Bardolph; lead the men away. [*Exeunt Bardolph, Recruits, &c.*] As I return, I will fetch off these justices: I do see the bottom of Justice Shallow. Lord, Lord, how subject we old men are to this vice of lying! This same starved justice hath done nothing but

---

l. 257 *Arthur's show* (a procession and archery show).
l. 258 *quiver*: lively.
l. 260 *rah, tah, tah* (loading).
l. 261 *'bounce'* (bangl).

l. 272 *I have spoke at a word*: I needn't say more.
l. 275 *fetch off*: fleece.
l. 278 *starved*: skinny.

prate to me of the wildness of his youth, and the feats
280 he hath done about Turnbull-street; and every third
word a lie, duer paid to the hearer than the Turk's
tribute. I do remember him at Clement's-inn, like a
man made after supper of a cheese-paring: when a' was
naked, he was, for all the world, like a fork'd radish,
with a head fantastically carved upon it with a knife; a'
was so forlorn, that his dimensions to any thick sight
were invisible: a' was the very genius of famine; yet
lecherous as a monkey ... a' came ever in the rearward
of the fashion; and sung those tunes ... that he heard
290 the carmen whistle, and sware they were his Fancies or
his Good-nights. And now is this Vice's dagger become
a Squire, and talks as familiarly of John o' Gaunt as if he
had been sworn brother to him; and I'll be sworn a' ne'er
saw him but once in the Tilt-yard; and then he burst his
head for crowding among the marshal's men. I saw it,
and told John o' Gaunt he beat his own name; for you
might have thrust him and all his apparel into an eel-
skin; the case of a treble haut-boy was a mansion for
him, a court: — and now has he land and beefs. Well,
300 I'll be acquainted with him, if I return; and it shall go
hard but I'll make him a philosopher's two stones to me:
if the young dace be a bait for the old pike, I see no
reason, in the law of nature, but I may snap at him. Let
time shape, and there an end.

---

l. 280 *Turnbull-street* (a haunt
of vice).
l. 281 *duer*: more surely.
l. 281 *Turk's tribute* (to the
Sultan).
l. 288 *lecherous*: immoral.
l. 291 *Vice's dagger*: comic turn.

l. 294 *Tilt-yard*: tournament
ground.
l. 296 *name* (of 'gaunt').
l. 298 *haut-boy*: oboe.
l. 301 *a philosopher's two stones*:
i.e. a gold-mine.

Some time later (after the war) at Shallow's House.

SHALLOW

1   By cock and pie, sir, you shall not away to-night. —
What, Davy, I say!,

FALSTAFF

You must excuse me, Master Robert Shallow.

SHALLOW

I will not excuse you; you shall not be excused; excuses
shall not be admitted; there is no excuse shall serve; you
shall not be excused. — Why, Davy!

Enter Davy.

DAVY

Here, sir.

SHALLOW

Davy, Davy, Davy, Davy, — let me see, Davy; let me
see, Davy; let me see: — yea, marry, William cook, bid
10 him come hither. — Sir John, you shall not be excused.

DAVY

Marry, sir, thus; those precepts cannot be served: and
again, sir, — shall we sow the headland with wheat?

SHALLOW

With red wheat, Davy. But for William cook: — are
there no young pigeons?

DAVY

Yes, sir. — Here is now the smith's note for shoeing and
plough-irons.

SHALLOW

Let it be cast, and paid. — Sir John, you shall not be
excused.

---

l. 11 *precepts*: writs.   l. 17 *cast*: checked.
l. 12 *headland*: border of the
field.

DAVY

Now, sir, a new link to the bucket must needs be had: —
20 and, sir, do you mean to stop any of William's wages,
about the sack he lost the other day at Hinckley fair?

SHALLOW

A' shall answer it. — Some pigeons, Davy, a couple of
short-legg'd hens, a joint of mutton, and any pretty
little tiny kickshaws, tell William cook.

DAVY

Doth the man of war stay all night, sir?

SHALLOW

Yea, Davy. I will use him well: a friend i' th' Court is
better than a penny in purse. Use his men well, Davy;
for they are arrant knaves, and will backbite.

DAVY

No worse than they are backbitten, sir; for they have
30 marvellous foul linen.

SHALLOW

Well conceited, Davy: — about thy business, Davy.

DAVY

I beseech you, sir, to countenance William Visor of
Woncot against Clement Perkes o' th' hill.

SHALLOW

There is many complaints, Davy, against that Visor:
that Visor is an arrant knave, on my knowledge.

DAVY

I grant your worship that he is a knave, sir; but yet,
God forbid, sir, but a knave should have some countenance at his friend's request. An honest man, sir, is
able to speak for himself, when a knave is not. I have

---

l. 19 *link*: chair.
l. 22 *answer*: pay for it.
l. 24 *kickshaws*: fancy dishes.
l. 29 *backbitten*: (by lice).

l. 31 *well conceited*: very witty
remark!
l. 32 *countenance*: favour

40 served your worship truly, sir, this eight years; and if
I cannot once or twice in a quarter bear out a knave
against an honest man, I have but a very little credit
with your worship. The knave is mine honest friend,
sir; therefore, I beseech your worship, let him be
countenanced.

SHALLOW

Go to; I say he shall have no wrong. Look about, Davy.
[*Exit Davy.*] Where are you, Sir John? Come, come,
come, off with your boots. — Give me your hand, Master
Bardolph.

BARDOLPH

50 I am glad to see your worship.

SHALLOW

I thank thee with all my heart, kind Master Bardolph: —
[*to the Page*] and welcome, my tall fellow. — Come, Sir
John.

FALSTAFF

I'll follow you, good Master Robert Shallow. [*Exit
Shallow.*] Bardolph, look to our horses. [*Exeunt
Bardolph and Page.*] If I were saw'd into quantities, I
should make four dozen of such bearded hermits'-
staves as Master Shallow ... I will devise matter enough
out of this Shallow to keep Prince Harry in continual
60 laughter. O, you shall see him laugh till his face be
like a wet cloak ill laid up!

SHALLOW [*within*]

Sir John!

FALSTAFF

I come, Master Shallow; I come, Master Shallow.

---

l. 41 *bear out*: support.

3

In Shallow's Orchard.

SHALLOW

1 NAY, you shall see my orchard, where, in an arbour, we
will eat a last year's pippin of my own graffing, with a
dish of caraways, and so forth: — come, cousin Silence:
— and then to bed.

FALSTAFF

'Fore God, you have here a goodly dwelling and a rich.

SHALLOW

Barren, barren, barren; beggars all, beggars all, Sir John:
— marry, good air! — Spread, Davy; spread, Davy: well
said, Davy.

FALSTAFF

This Davy serves you for good uses; he is your serving-
10 man and your husband.

SHALLOW

A good varlet, a good varlet, a very good varlet, Sir
John: — by the mass, I have drunk too much sack at
supper: — a good varlet. Now sit down, now sit down:
— come, cousin.

SILENCE

Ah, sirrah! quoth-a, — we shall

[*Singing.*

Do nothing but eat, and make good cheer,
And praise God for the merry year;
When flesh is cheap and females dear,
And lusty lads roam here and there
20   So merrily,
And ever among so merrily.

---

l. 3 *caraways*: seed-cakes.
l. 3 (*Silence* is now rather 'merry').
l. 7 *spread*: lay the table.

l. 7 *well said*: good!
l. 10 *husband*: steward.
l. 12 *sack*: wine.

FALSTAFF

There's a merry heart! — Good Master Silence, I'll give
you a health for that anon.

SHALLOW

Give Master Bardolph some wine, Davy.

DAVY

Sweet sir, sit; I'll be with you anon; most sweet sir, sit.
— Master page, good master page, sit. — Proface! What
you want in meat, we'll have in drink: but you must
bear; — the heart's all.   [*Exit.*

SHALLOW

Be merry, Master Bardolph; — and, my little soldier
30   there, be merry.

SILENCE [*singing*]

Be merry, be merry, my wife has all;
For women are shrews, both short and tall:
'Tis merry in hall when beards wag all,
    And welcome merry Shrove-tide.
Be merry, be merry.

FALSTAFF

I did not think Master Silence had been a man of this
mettle.

SILENCE

Who, I? I have been merry twice and once ere now.

Enter Davy.

DAVY

There's a dish of leather-coats for you.

                    [*Setting them before Bardolph.*

SHALLOW

40   Davy, —

---

l. 26 *proface!*: good health!   l. 39 *leather-coats*: russet apples
l. 28 *bear*: excuse us.   (thick skins).

DAVY

Your worship? — [*to Bardolph*] I'll be with you straight.
— A cup of wine, sir?

SILENCE [*singing*]

A cup of wine that's brisk and fine,
And drink unto the leman mine;
And a merry heart lives long-a.

FALSTAFF

Well said, Master Silence.

SILENCE

And we shall be merry; — now comes in the sweet o'
th' night.

FALSTAFF

Health and long life to you, Master Silence!

SILENCE [*singing*]

50   Fill the cup, and let it come;
I'll pledge you a mile to the bottom.

SHALLOW

Honest Bardolph, welcome: if thou want'st any thing,
and wilt not call, beshrew thy heart. — [*To the Page*]
Welcome, my little tiny thief, and welcome indeed too.
— I'll drink to Master Bardolph, and to all the cavaleroes
about London.

DAVY

I hope to see London once ere I die.

BARDOLPH

An I might see you there, Davy, —

SHALLOW

By the mass, you'll crack a quart together, — ha! will
60 you not, Master Bardolph?

BARDOLPH

Yea, sir, in a pottle-pot.

---

l. 44 *leman*: sweetheart.   l. 61 *pottle*: 2 quart.
l. 59 *crack*: share.

SHALLOW

By God's liggens, I thank thee: — the knave will stick
by thee, I can assure thee that: a' will not out; he is
true bred.

BARDOLPH

And I'll stick by him, sir.

SHALLOW

Why, there spoke a king. Lack nothing: be merry!

King Henry IV, Part Two, III. 2, V. 1, 3

ALARUMS AND EXCURSIONS

*King Henry V is about to assault the city of Harfleur. In his
army are many contrasting types: the cowardly hangers-on, Nym,
Bardolph and Pistol; the sturdy Scot, Jamy; the touchy
Irishman, Macmorris; the zealous and efficient Welshman,
Fluellen; the warlike knights and the good yeomen of England.
It is 'God for Harry, England, and Saint George!'*

Before a breach blown in the walls of Harfleur.

KING HENRY

1 ONCE more unto the breach, dear friends, once more;
Or close the wall up with our English dead!
In peace there's nothing so becomes a man
As modest stillness and humility:
But when the blast of war blows in our ears,
Then imitate the action of the tiger;
Stiffen the sinews, summon up the blood,
Disguise fair nature with hard-favour'd rage:

---

l. 62 *liggens* (meaning un-   l. 8 *hard-favour'd*: ugly.
known).

127

Then lend the eye a terrible aspect;
10   Let it pry through the portage of the head
Like the brass cannon; let the brow o'erwhelm it
As fearfully as doth a galled rock
O'erhang and jutty his confounded base,
Swill'd with the wild and wasteful ocean.
Now set the teeth, and stretch the nostril wide;
Hold hard the breath, and bend up every spirit
To his full height! — On, on, you noble English,
Whose blood is fet from fathers of war-proof! —
Fathers that, like so many Alexanders,
20   Have in these parts from morn till even fought,
And sheath'd their swords for lack of argument: —
Dishonour not your mothers; now attest
That those whom you call'd fathers did beget you!
Be copy now to men of grosser blood,
And teach them how to war! — And you, good yeomen,
Whose limbs were made in England, show us here
The mettle of your pasture; let us swear
That you are worth your breeding: which I doubt not;
For there is none of you so mean and base,
30   That hath not noble lustre in your eyes.
I see you stand like greyhounds in the slips,
Straining upon the start. The game's afoot:
Follow your spirit; and, upon this charge,
Cry 'God for Harry, England, and Saint George!'
               [*They rush forward to attack the walls.*
        Enter Nym, Bardolph, Pistol, and Boy.

---

l. 10 *portage*: port-hole.
l. 12 *galled*: chafed by the sea.
l. 13 *confounded*: worn.
l. 18 *fet*: fetched.
l. 19 *Alexanders* (The Great, the famous conqueror).
l. 21 *argument*: enemies.

l. 22 *attest*: prove.
l. 24 *grosser*: coarser.
l. 27 *mettle*: quality.
l. 32 *the game's afoot* (for the hounds to course).
l. 33 *upon*: in.

BARDOLPH

On, on, on, on, on! to the breach, to the breach!

NYM

Pray thee, corporal, stay: the knocks are too hot; and,
for mine own part, I have not a case of lives: the humour
of it is too hot, that is the very plain-song of it.

PISTOL

The plain-song is most just; for humours do abound;
40 Knocks go and come; God's vassals drop and die;
> And sword and shield,
> In bloody field,
> Doth win immortal fame.

BOY

Would I were in an alehouse in London! I would give
all my fame for a pot of ale and safety.

PISTOL

And I:
> If wishes would prevail with me,
> My purpose should not fail with me,
> But thither would I hie.

BOY

50 > As duly, but not as truly,
> As bird doth sing on bough.
> *Enter Fluellen, a Welsh Captain.*

FLUELLEN

Got's plood! — Up to the preaches, you rascals! will you
not up to the preaches?   [*Driving them forward.*

PISTOL

Be merciful, great duke, to men of mould!

---

l. 37 *case*: set.
l. 37 *the humour of it is too hot,
that is the very plain-song*:
it's too risky: that's what I feel
about it.

l. 50 *duly*: rightly.
l. 50 *truly*: tunefully.
l. 54 *men of mould*: mortal men.

Abate thy rage, abate thy manly rage!
Abate thy rage, great duke!
Good bawcock, bate thy rage! use lenity, sweet chuck!

NYM

These be good humours! — your honour runs bad humours.

[Exeunt Nym, Bardolph, and Pistol, driven by Fluellen.

BOY

60 As young as I am, I have observed these three swashers. I am boy to them all three: but all they three, though they would serve me, could not be man to me; for, indeed, three such antics do not amount to a man. For Bardolph, — he is white-liver'd and red-faced; by the means whereof a' faces it out, but fights not. For Pistol, — he hath a killing tongue and a quiet sword; by the means whereof a' breaks words, and keeps whole weapons. For Nym, — he hath heard that men of few words are the best men; and therefore he scorns to say
70 his prayers, lest a' should be thought a coward: but his few bad words are match'd with as few good deeds; for a' never broke any man's head but his own, and that was against a post when he was drunk. They will steal any thing, and call it 'purchase'. Bardolph stole a lute-case, bore it twelve leagues, and sold it for three-half-pence. Nym and Bardolph are sworn brothers in filching; and in Calais they stole a fire-shovel: I knew by that piece of service the men would carry coals. They would have me as familiar with men's pockets as their gloves
80 or their handkerchers: which makes much against my manhood, if I should take from another's pocket to put

---

l. 57 *good bawcock*: my fine fellow.
l. 57 *sweet chuck*: my dear man.
l. 58 *humours*: moods.
l. 58 *your honour* (Fluellen).

l. 60 *swashers*: bullies.
l. 63 *antics*: comics.
l. 64 *white-liver'd*: cowardly.
l. 78 *carry coals*: do dirty work.

into mine; for it is plain pocketing-up of wrongs. I must leave them, and seek some better service: their villainy goes against my weak stomach, and therefore I must cast it up.   *[Exit.*

Enter Fluellen, Gower (an Officer) following

GOWER

Captain Fluellen, you must come presently to the mines; the Duke of Gloster would speak with you.

FLUELLEN

To the mines! tell you the duke, it is not so goot to come to the mines; for, look you, the mines is not
90 according to the disciplines of the war: the concavities of it is not sufficient; for, look you, th' athversary — you may discuss unto the duke, look you — is digt himself four yard under the countermines: by Cheshu, I think a' will plow up all, if there is not petter directions.

GOWER

The Duke of Gloster, to whom the order of the siege is given, is altogether directed by an Irishman, — a very valiant gentleman, i' faith.

FLUELLEN

It is Captain Macmorris, is it not?

GOWER

I think it be.

FLUELLEN

100 By Cheshu, he is an ass, as in the 'orld: I will verify as much in his peard: he has no more directions in the true disciplines of the wars, look you, of the Roman disciplines, than is a puppy-dog.

---

l. 85 *cast*: give.

l. 86 *presently*: now.

l. 86 *mines* (dug under the walls for explosive charges).

l. 90 *concavities*: depth.

l. 93 *Cheshu*: Jesu.

GOWER

Here a' comes; and the Scots captain, Captain Jamy, with him.

FLUELLEN

Captain Jamy is a marvellous falorous gentleman, that is certain; and of great expedition and knowledge in th' auncient wars, upon my particular knowledge of his directions: by Cheshu, he will maintain his argument as
110 well as any military man in the 'orld, in the disciplines of the pristine wars of the Romans.

Enter Macmorris and Jamy (Irish and Scotch Captains).

JAMY

I say gude-day, Captain Fluellen.

FLUELLEN

Got-den to your worship, goot Captain Jamy.

GOWER

How now, Captain Macmorris! have you quit the mines? have the pioners given o'er?

MACMORRIS

By Chrish, la, tish ill done; the work ish give over, the trompet sound the retreat. By my hand, I swear, and my father's soul, the work ish ill done; it ish give over: I would have blow'd up the town, so Chrish save me,
120 la, in an hour: O, tish ill done, tish ill done; by my hand, tish ill done!

FLUELLEN

Captain Macmorris, I peseech you now, will you voutsafe me, look you, a few disputations with you, as partly touching or concerning the disciplines of the war, the Roman wars, in the way of argument, look you, and friendly communication; partly to satisfy my opinion, and partly for the satisfaction, look you, of my mind, as

---

l. 109 *directions*: orders.   l. 115 *pioners*: sappers.
l. 111 *pristine*: early.   l. 116 *Chrish*: Christ.

touching the direction of the military discipline; that is
the point.

JAMY

130 It sall be very gude, gude feith, gude captains baith:
and I sall quit you with gude leve, as I may pick
occasion; that sall I, marry.

MACMORRIS

It is no time to discourse, so Chrish save me: the day is
hot, and the weather, and the wars, and the king, and
the dukes: it is no time to discourse. The town is
beseecht, and the trompet call us to the breach; and we
talk, and, be Chrish, do nothing: 'tis shame for us all: so
God sa' me, 'tis shame to stand still; it is shame, by my
hand: and there is throats to be cut, and works to be
140 done; and there ish nothing done, so Chrish sa' me, la.

JAMY

By the mess, ere theise eyes of mine take themselves to
slomber, ay'll do gude service, or ay'll lig i' th' grund
for it; ay, or go to death; and ay'll pay't as valorously as
I may, that sall I suerly do, that is the breff and the long.
Marry, I wad full fain heard some question 'tween you tway.

FLUELLEN

Captain Macmorris, I think, look you, under your
correction, there is not many of your nation —

MACMORRIS

Of my nation! What ish my nation? Ish a villain, and a
bastard, and a knave, and a rascal — What ish my
150 nation? Who talks of my nation?

FLUELLEN

Look you, if you take the matter otherwise than is
meant, Captain Macmorris, peradventure I shall think
you do not use me with that affability as in discretion

---

l. 131 *quit*: answer.   l. 153 *affability*: good fellow-
ship.

you ought to use me, look you; being as goot a man as yourself, both in the disciplines of war, and in the derivation of my birth, and in other particularities.

MACMORRIS

I do not know you so good a man as myself: so Chrish save me, I will cut off your head.

GOWER

Gentlemen both, you will mistake each other.

JAMY

160 A! that's a foul fault.   [*A parley sounded.*

GOWER

The town sounds a parley.

FLUELLEN

Captain Macmorris, when there is more petter opportunity to be required, look you, I will be so pold as to tell you I know the disciplines of war; and there is an end.

2

The Governor and some Citizens on the inner walls. Enter King Henry and his troops before the gates.

KING HENRY

1   How yet resolves the governor of the town?
This is the latest parle we will admit:
Therefore, to our best mercy give yourselves;
Or, like to men proud of destruction,
Defy us to our worst: for, as I am a soldier
(A name that, in my thoughts, becomes me best),
If I begin the battery once again,
I will not leave the half-achiev'd Harfleur
Till in her ashes she lie buried.
10 The gates of mercy shall be all shut up;

---

l. 1 *resolves*: decides.

And the flesh'd soldier, — rough and hard of heart, —
In liberty of bloody hand shall range
With conscience wide as hell; mowing like grass
Your fresh-fair virgins and your flowering infants.
What is it then to me, if impious war, —
Array'd in flames, like to the prince of fiends, —
Do, with his smirch'd complexion, all fell feats
Enlink'd to waste and desolation?
What is't to me, when you yourselves are cause,
20 If your pure maidens fall into the hand
Of hot and forcing violation?
What rein can hold licentious wickedness
When down the hill he holds his fierce career?
We may as bootless spend our vain command
Upon th' enraged soldiers in their spoil,
As send precepts to the Leviathan
To come ashore. Therefore, you men of Harfleur,
Take pity of your town and of your people,
Whiles yet my soldiers are in my command;
30 Whiles yet the cool and temperate wind of grace
O'erblows the filthy and contagious clouds
Of heady murder, spoil, and villainy.
If not, why, in a moment, look to see
The blind and bloody soldier with foul hand
Defile the locks of your shrill-shrieking daughters;
Your fathers taken by the silver beards,
And their most reverend heads dash'd to the walls;
Your naked infants spitted upon pikes,
Whiles the mad mothers with their howls confused
40 Do break the clouds, as did the wives of Jewry
At Herod's bloody-hunting slaughtermen.
What say you? will you yield, and this avoid?

---

l. 21 *violation*: insult.   l. 26 *Leviathan*: sea-monster.
l. 24 *bootless*: uselessly.   l. 31 *contagious*: infectious.

Or, guilty in defence, be thus destroy'd?

GOVERNOR OF HARFLEUR

Our expectation hath this day an end:
The Dauphin, whom of succour we entreated,
Returns us that his powers are yet not ready
To raise so great a siege. Therefore, dread king,
We yield our town and lives to thy soft mercy.
Enter our gates; dispose of us and ours;
50 For we no longer are defensible.

KING HENRY

Open your gates. — Come, uncle Exeter,
Go you and enter Harfleur; there remain,
And fortify it strongly 'gainst the French:
Use mercy to them all. For us, dear uncle, —
The winter coming on, and sickness growing
Upon our soldiers, — we will retire to Calais.
To-night in Harfleur will we be your guest;
To-morrow for the march are we address'd.

King Henry V, III. 1, 2, 3

THE EVE OF AGINCOURT

*The English Army, greatly outnumbered, faces the prospect of
defeat. King Henry, as anxious as any of his men, is walking
unattended among the tents.*

*The English Camp at Agincourt. Enter King Henry, Bedford,
and Gloster.*

KING HENRY

1 GLOSTER, 'tis true that we are in great danger;
The greater therefore should our courage be. —

---

l. 45 *Dauphin*: Crown Prince.   l. 58 *address'd*: ready.

Good morrow, brother Bedford. — God Almighty!
There is some soul of goodness in things evil,
Would men observingly distil it out;
For our bad neighbour makes us early stirrers,
Which is both healthful and good husbandry:
Besides, they are our outward consciences,
And preachers to us all; admonishing
10   That we should dress us fairly for our end.
Thus may we gather honey from the weed,
And make a moral of the devil himself.
                Enter Erpingham.
Good morrow, old Sir Thomas Erpingham:
A good soft pillow for that good white head
Were better than a churlish turf of France.

          ERPINGHAM

Not so, my liege: this lodging likes me better,
Since I may say, 'Now lie I like a king.'

          KING HENRY

'Tis good for men to love their present pains
Upon example; so the spirit is eased:
20   And when the mind is quicken'd, out of doubt
The organs, though defunct and dead before,
Break up their drowsy grave, and newly move
With casted slough and fresh legerity.
Lend me thy cloak, Sir Thomas. — Brothers both,
Commend me to the princes in our camp;
Do my good morrow to them; and anon
Desire them all to my pavilion.

          GLOSTER

We shall, my liege.

          ERPINGHAM

Shall I attend your Grace?

---

l. 7 *husbandry*: management.   l. 23 *legerity*: liveliness.
l. 23 *slough*: snake's skin.

KING HENRY

No, my good knight;
30 Go with my brothers to my lords of England:
I and my bosom must debate awhile,
And then I would no other company.

ERPINGHAM

The Lord in heaven bless thee, noble Harry!

[*Exeunt Gloster, Bedford, and Erpingham.*

KING HENRY

God-a-mercy, old heart! thou speak'st cheerfully.

Enter Pistol

PISTOL

Qui va là?

KING HENRY

A friend.

PISTOL

Discuss unto me; art thou officer?
Or art thou base, common, and popular?

KING HENRY

I am a gentleman of a company.

PISTOL

40 Trail'st thou the puissant pike?

KING HENRY

Even so. What are you?

PISTOL

As good a gentleman as the emperor.

KING HENRY

Then you are a better than the king.

PISTOL

The king's a bawcock, and a heart of gold,
A lad of life, an imp of fame;

---

l. 39 *gentleman of a company:*
gentleman-volunteer in the
ranks.

l. 40 *puissant:* powerful.
l. 44 *bawcock:* fine fellow.
l. 45 *imp:* child.

Of parents good, of fist most valiant:
I kiss his dirty shoe, and from heart-string
I love the lovely bully. — What is thy name?

KING HENRY

Harry *le Roy*.

PISTOL

50 Le Roy!
A Cornish name: art thou of Cornish crew?

KING HENRY

No, I am a Welshman.

PISTOL

Know'st thou Fluellen?

KING HENRY

Yes.

PISTOL

Tell him, I'll knock his leek about his pate
Upon Saint Davy's day.

KING HENRY

Do not you wear your dagger in your cap that day, lest
he knock that about yours.

PISTOL

Art thou his friend?

KING HENRY

60 And his kinsman too.

PISTOL

The figo for thee, then!

KING HENRY

I thank you: God be with you!

PISTOL

My name is Pistol call'd.   [*Exit*.

KING HENRY

It sorts well with your fierceness.

---

l. 55 *leek*: Welsh national emblem.   l. 61 *The figo for thee* (an insult)

Enter Fluellen and Gower, meeting.

GOWER

Captain Fluellen!

FLUELLEN

So! in the name of Cheshu Christ, speak lower. It is
the greatest admiration in the universal 'orld, when the
true and auncient prerogatifs and laws of the wars is
not kept: if you would take the pains but to examine the
70   wars of Pompey the Great, you shall find, I warrant you,
that there is no tiddle-taddle nor pibble-pabble in
Pompey's camp; I warrant you, you shall find the
ceremonies of the wars, and the cares of it, and the
forms of it, and the sobriety of it, and the modesty of it,
to be otherwise.

GOWER

Why, the enemy is loud; you heard him all night.

FLUELLEN

If the enemy is an ass, and a fool, and a prating coxcomb,
is it meet, think you, that we should also, look you, be
an ass, and a fool, and a prating coxcomb, — in your
80   own conscience, now?

GOWER

I will speak lower.

FLUELLEN

I pray you, and peseech you, that you will.

                    [Exeunt Gower and Fluellen.

KING HENRY

Though it appear a little out of fashion,
There is much care and valour in this Welshman.

*Enter three soldiers, John Bates, Alexander Court, and Michael
Williams.*

---

l. 68 *prerogatifs*: privileges.

ALEXANDER COURT

Brother John Bates, is not that the morning which breaks yonder?

JOHN BATES

I think it be: but we have no great cause to desire the approach of day.

MICHAEL WILLIAMS

90 We see yonder the beginning of the day, but I think we shall never see the end of it. — Who goes there?

KING HENRY

A friend.

MICHAEL WILLIAMS

Under what captain serve you?

KING HENRY

Under Sir Thomas Erpingham.

MICHAEL WILLIAMS

A good old commander and a most kind gentleman: I pray you, what thinks he of our estate?

KING HENRY

Even as men wrack'd upon a sand, that look to be wash'd off the next tide.

JOHN BATES

He hath not told his thought to the king?

KING HENRY

100 No; nor is it meet he should. For, though I speak it to you, I think the king is but a man, as I am: the violet smells to him as it doth to me; the element shows to him as it doth to me; all his senses have but human conditions: his ceremonies laid by, in his nakedness he appears but a man; and though his affections are higher mounted than ours, yet, when they stoop, they stoop with the like wing. Therefore when he sees reason of

---

l. 101 *element*: sky.　　　　l. 104 *affections*: desires.
l. 103 *conditions*: characteristics.

fears, as we do, his fears, out of doubt, be of the same relish as ours are: yet, in reason, no man should possess him with any appearance of fear, lest he, by showing it, 110 should dishearten his army.

JOHN BATES

He may show what outward courage he will; but I believe, as cold a night as 'tis, he could wish himself in Thames up to the neck; — and so I would he were, and I by him, at all adventures, so we were quit here.

KING HENRY

By my troth, I will speak my conscience of the king: I think he would not wish himself any where but where he is.

JOHN BATES

Then I would he were here alone; so should he be sure to be ransom'd, and a many poor men's lives saved.

KING HENRY

120 I dare say you love him not so ill, to wish him here alone, howsoever you speak this, to feel other men's minds: methinks I could not die any where so contented as in the king's company, — his cause being just, and his quarrel honourable.

MICHAEL WILLIAMS

That's more than we know.

JOHN BATES

Ay, or more than we should seek after; for we know enough, if we know we are the king's subjects: if his cause be wrong, our obedience to the king wipes the crime of it out of us.

MICHAEL WILLIAMS

130 But if the cause be not good, the king himself hath a heavy reckoning to make, when all those legs and arms

---

l. 108 *relish*: taste. l. 108 *possess him with*: cause him.

and heads, chopp'd off in battle, shall join together at the latter day, and cry all, 'We died at such a place'; some swearing; some crying for a surgeon; some upon their wives left poor behind them; some, upon the debts they owe; some upon their children rawly left. I am afeard there are few die well that die in battle, for how can they charitably dispose of any thing, when blood is their argument? Now, if these men do not die well, it
140 will be a black matter for the king that led them to it; who to disobey were against all proportion of subjection.

KING HENRY

So, if a son, that is by his father sent about merchandise, do sinfully miscarry upon the sea, the imputation of his wickedness, by your rule, should be imposed upon his father that sent him: or if a servant, under his master's command transporting a sum of money, be assail'd by robbers, and die in many irreconciled iniquities, you may call the business of the master the author of the servant's damnation: — but this is not so: the king is not
150 bound to answer the particular endings of his soldiers, the father of his son, nor the master of his servant; for they purpose not their death, when they purpose their services. Besides, there is no king, be his cause never so spotless, if it come to the arbitrement of swords, can try it out with all unspotted soldiers: some peradventure have on them the guilt of premeditated and contrived murder; some, of beguiling virgins with the broken seals of perjury; some, making the wars their bulwark, that have before gored the gentle bosom of peace with

---

l. 136 *rawly*: unprovided for.
l. 138 *dispose of*: settle.
l. 141 *all proportion of subjection*: a subject's duty.

l. 143 *imputation of*: responsibility for.
l. 154 *arbitrement*: decision.
l. 157 *beguiling*: deceiving.
l. 158 *perjury*: false promises.

160 pillage and robbery. Now, if these men have defeated the law and outrun native punishment, though they can outstrip men, they have no wings to fly from God: war is his beadle, war is his vengeance; so that here men are punish'd for before-breach of the king's laws in now the king's quarrel: where they fear'd the death, they have borne life away; and where they would be safe, they perish: then if they die unprovided, no more is the king guilty of their damnation, than he was before guilty of those impieties for the which they are now visited.

170 Every subject's duty is the king's; but every subject's soul is his own. Therefore should every soldier in the wars do as every sick man in his bed, — wash every mote out of his conscience: and dying so, death is to him advantage; or not dying, the time was blessedly lost wherein such preparation was gain'd: and in him that escapes, it were not sin to think that, making God so free an offer, he let him outlive that day to see his greatness, and to teach others how they should prepare.

MICHAEL WILLIAMS

'Tis certain, every man that dies ill, the ill upon his own 180 head, — the king is not to answer it.

JOHN BATES

I do not desire he should answer for me; and yet I determine to fight lustily for him.

KING HENRY

I myself heard the king say he would not be ransom'd.

MICHAEL WILLIAMS

Ay, he said so, to make us fight cheerfully: but when our throats are cut, he may be ransom'd, and we ne'er the wiser.

---

l. 163 *beadle*: officer.   l. 173 *mote*: speck.

KING HENRY

If I live to see it, I will never trust his word after.

MICHAEL WILLIAMS

'Mass, you'll pay him then! That's a perilous shot out of an elder-gun, that a poor and a private displeasure can do against a monarch! you may as well go about to turn the sun to ice with fanning in his face with a peacock's feather. You'll never trust his word after! come, 'tis a foolish saying.

KING HENRY

Your reproof is something too round: I should be angry with you, if the time were convenient.

MICHAEL WILLIAMS

Let it be a quarrel between us, if you live.

KING HENRY

I embrace it.

MICHAEL WILLIAMS

How shall I know thee again?

KING HENRY

Give me any gage of thine, and I will wear it in my bonnet: then, if ever thou darest acknowledge it, I will make it my quarrel.

MICHAEL WILLIAMS

Here's my glove: give me another of thine.

KING HENRY

There.

MICHAEL WILLIAMS

This will I also wear in my cap: if ever thou come to me and say, after to-morrow, 'This is my glove,' by this hand, I will take thee a box on the ear.

---

l. 188 *pay*: pay him out (if he breaks it).

l. 189 *elder-gun*: popgun.

l. 199 *gage*: sign that you will maintain your challenge.

KING HENRY

If ever I live to see it, I will challenge it.

MICHAEL WILLIAMS

Thou darest as well be hang'd.

KING HENRY

Well, I will do it, though I take thee in the king's
210 company.

MICHAEL WILLIAMS

Keep thy word: fare thee well.

JOHN BATES

Be friends, you English fools, be friends: we have
French quarrels enow, if you could tell how to reckon.

KING HENRY

Indeed, the French may lay twenty French crowns to
one, they will beat us; for they bear them on their
shoulders: but it is no English treason to cut French
crowns; and to-morrow the king himself will be a
clipper.   [*Exeunt Soldiers.*

Upon the king! — let us our lives, our souls,
220 Our debts, our careful wives,
Our children, and our sins, lay on the king!
We must bear all. O hard condition,
Twin-born with greatness, subject to the breath
Of every fool, whose sense no more can feel
But his own wringing!
What infinite heart's-ease must kings neglect,
That private men enjoy!
And what have kings, that privates have not too,
Save ceremony, — save general ceremony?
230 And what art thou, thou idol ceremony?
What kind of god art thou, that suffer'st more

---

l. 214 *crowns*: crown-pieces.   l. 217 *crowns*: crown pieces (or
l. 216 *cut*: clip.   heads!).
                                   l. 225 *wringing*: stomach ache.

Of mortal griefs than do thy worshippers?
What are thy rents? what are thy comings-in?
O ceremony, show me but thy worth!
What is thy soul of adoration?
Art thou aught else but place, degree, and form,
Creating awe and fear in other men?
Wherein thou art less happy being fear'd
Than they in fearing?
240   What drink'st thou oft, instead of homage sweet,
But poison'd flattery? O, be sick, great greatness,
And bid thy ceremony give thee cure!
Think'st thou the fiery fever will go out
With titles blown from adulation?
Will it give place to flexure and low bending?
Canst thou, when thou command'st the beggar's knee,
Command the health of it? No, thou proud dream,
That play'st so subtly with a king's repose:
I am a king that find thee; and I know
250   'Tis not the balm, the sceptre, and the ball,
The sword, the mace, the crown imperial,
The intertissued robe of gold and pearl,
The farced title running 'fore the king,
The throne he sits on, nor the tide of pomp
That beats upon the high shore of this world, —
No, not all these, thrice-gorgeous ceremony,
Not all these, laid in bed majestical,
Can sleep so soundly as the wretched slave,
Who, with a body fill'd and vacant mind,
260   Gets him to rest, cramm'd with distressful bread;

---

l. 233 *comings-in*: income.
l. 235 *soul of adoration*: the real nature of thy worship.
l. 236 *degree*: rank.
l. 244 *adulation*: flattery.

l. 245 *flexure*: bowing.
l. 250 *balm*: holy oil.
l. 250 *ball*: orb.
l. 253 *farced*: wordy.

Never sees horrid night, the child of hell;
But, like a lackey, from the rise to set,
Sweats in the eye of Phœbus, and all night
Sleeps in Elysium; next day, after dawn,
Doth rise, and help Hyperion to his horse;
And follows so the ever-running year,
With profitable labour, to his grave:
And, but for ceremony, such a wretch,
Winding up days with toil and nights with sleep,
270 Had the fore-hand and vantage of a king.
The slave, a member of the country's peace,
Enjoys it; but in gross brain little wots
What watch the king keeps to maintain the peace,
Whose hours the peasant best advantages.

           Enter Erpingham.

ERPINGHAM

My lord, your nobles, jealous of your absence,
Seek through your camp to find you.

KING HENRY

                         Good old knight,

Collect them all together at my tent:
I'll be before thee.

ERPINGHAM

        I shall do 't, my lord.   [*Exit.*

KING HENRY

O God of battles! steel my soldiers' hearts;
280 Possess them not with fear; take from them now
The sense of reckoning, if th' opposed numbers
Pluck their hearts from them! — Not to-day, O Lord,
O, not to-day, think not upon the fault

---

l. 263 *in the eye of Phœbus:*
sunshine.
l. 264 *Elysium:* bliss.

l. 265 *Hyperion:* the sun-god.
l. 274 *advantages:* profits.
l. 275 *jealous of:* anxious at.

My father made in compassing the crown!
I Richard's body have interred new;
And on it have bestow'd more contrite tears
Than from it issued forced drops of blood:
Five hundred poor I have in yearly pay,
Who twice a-day their wither'd hands hold up
290 Toward heaven, to pardon blood; and I have built
Two chantries, where the sad and solemn priests
Sing still for Richard's soul. More will I do;
Though all that I can do is nothing worth,
Since that my penitence comes after all,
Imploring pardon.

Enter Gloster.

GLOSTER

My liege!

KING HENRY

My brother Gloster's voice? — Ay;
I know thy errand, I will go with thee: —
The day, my friends, and all things stay for me.

King Henry V, IV. 1

ADMIRABLE FOOLING

*The Lady Olivia's jovial kinsman Sir Toby Belch has brought
into the house a foolish knight, Sir Andrew Aguecheek, who
hopes to marry the lady. Olivia's maid and her jester are
always ready to join the two knights in a carouse, but Malvolio,
the ambitious, conceited, and puritanical steward, by no means
approves of what goes on in the small hours.*

---

l. 284 *My father* (King
Henry IV had seized the
crown from King Richard II).

l. 286 *contrite*: penitent.

l. 291 *chantries*: chapels.

ADMIRABLE FOOLING

In Olivia's House. Enter Sir Toby and Sir Andrew.

SIR TOBY

1 APPROACH, Sir Andrew: not to be a-bed after midnight is to be up betimes; and *diluculo surgere*, thou know'st, —

SIR ANDREW

Nay, by my troth, I know not: but I know, to be up late is to be up late.

SIR TOBY

A false conclusion: I hate it as an unfill'd can. To be up after midnight, and to go to bed then, is early: so that to go to bed after midnight is to go to bed betimes. Does not our life consist of the four elements?

SIR ANDREW

Faith, so they say; but, I think, it rather consists of
10 eating and drinking.

SIR TOBY

Th' art a scholar: let us therefore eat and drink. — Marian, I say! a stoup of wine!

SIR ANDREW

Here comes the fool, i' faith.

Enter Clown. *

CLOWN

How now, my hearts! did you never see the picture of We Three?

SIR TOBY

Welcome, ass. Now let's have a catch.

SIR ANDREW

By my troth, the fool has an excellent breast. I had rather than forty shillings I had such a leg, and so sweet a breath to sing, as the fool has. In sooth, thou

---

l. 2 *diluculo surgere*: to get up early (is good for you).
l. 8 *of the four elements*: earth, air, fire, water.

l. 12 *stoup*: flagon.
* Olivia's jester.
l. 16 *catch*: song.
l. 17 *breast*: voice.

20 wast in very gracious fooling last night, when thou
spokest of Pigrogromitus, of the Vapians passing the
equinoctial of Queubus: 'twas very good, i' faith. I
sent thee sixpence for thy leman: hadst it?

CLOWN

I did impeticos thy gratillity; for Malvolio's nose is no
whipstock; my lady has a white hand, and the Myrmidons are no bottle-ale houses.

SIR ANDREW

Excellent! why, this is the best fooling, when all is done.
Now, a song.

SIR TOBY

Come on; there is sixpence for you: let's have a song.

SIR ANDREW

30 There's a testril of me too; if one knight give a —

CLOWN

Would you have a love-song, or a song of good life?

SIR TOBY

A love-song, a love-song.

SIR ANDREW

Ay, ay: I care not for good life.

CLOWN [sings]

O mistress mine, where are you roaming?
O, stay and hear; your true-love's coming,
    That can sing both high and low:
Trip no further, pretty sweeting;
Journeys end in lovers' meeting,
    Every wise man's son doth know.

---

l. 21 *Pigrogromitus*, etc. (all nonsense!).
l. 23 *leman*: sweetheart.
l. 24 *I did impeticos thy gratillity; for Malvolio's nose is no
whipstock; my lady has a white
hand, and the Myrmidons are*
no bottle-ale houses: I pocketed
your stingy little tip myself,
for Malvolio was on the look-
out. My girl is really high class
and our tavern isn't a common
drink-shop.
l. 30 *testril*: sixpence.

SIR ANDREW

40 Excellent good, i' faith.

SIR TOBY

Good, good.

CLOWN

What is love? 'tis not hereafter;
Present mirth hath present laughter;
    What's to come is still unsure:
In delay there lies no plenty;
Then come kiss me, sweet-and-twenty,
    Youth's a stuff will not endure.

SIR ANDREW

A mellifluous voice, as I am true knight.

SIR TOBY

A contagious breath.

SIR ANDREW

50 Very sweet and contagious, i' faith.

SIR TOBY

To hear by the nose, it is dulcet in contagion. But shall
we make the welkin dance indeed? shall we rouse the
night-owl in a catch that will draw three souls out of
one weaver? shall we do that?

SIR ANDREW

An you love me, let's do 't: I am dog at a catch.

CLOWN

By'r lady, sir, and some dogs will catch well.

SIR ANDREW

Most certain. Let our catch be, 'Thou knave.'

---

l. 48 *mellifluous*: honeyed.
l. 49 *contagious breath*: catchy song.
l. 50 *contagious*: infectious.

l. 51 *dulcet*: sweet.
l. 53 *three souls out of one weaver* (some weavers were very pious).

CLOWN

'Hold thy peace, thou knave,' knight? I shall be constrain'd in 't to call thee knave, knight.

SIR ANDREW

60 'Tis not the first time I have constrain'd one to call me knave. Begin, fool: it begins, 'Hold thy peace.'

CLOWN

I shall never begin, if I hold my peace.

SIR ANDREW

Good, i' faith. Come, begin. [*Catch sung: 'Hold thy peace, thou knave knight'*]

Enter Maria.

MARIA

What a caterwauling do you keep here! If my lady have not call'd up her steward Malvolio, and bid him turn you out of doors, never trust me.

SIR TOBY

My lady's a Cataian, we are politicians, Malvolio's a Peg-a-Ramsey, and 'Three merry men be we.' Am not I consanguineous? am I not of her blood? Tilly-vally, 70 lady! [*Sings*] 'There dwelt a man in Babylon, lady, lady!'

CLOWN

Beshrew me, the knight's in admirable fooling.

SIR ANDREW

Ay, he does well enough if he be disposed, and so do I too: he does it with a better grace, but I do it more natural.

SIR TOBY [*singing*]

'O, the twelfth day of December, —'

MARIA

For the love o' God, peace!

---

l. 67 *Cataian*: cheat.   l. 69 *consanguineous*: related.
l. 67 *politicians*: schemers.   l. 69 *Tilly-vally*: nonsense!
l. 68 *Peg-a-Ramsey*: joke.

Enter Malvolio.

MALVOLIO

My masters, are you mad? or what are you? Have you
no wit, manners, nor honesty, but to gabble like tinkers
at this time of night? Do ye make an ale-house of my
80 lady's house that ye squeak out your cosiers' catches
without any mitigation or remorse of voice? Is there no
respect of place, persons, nor time, in you?

SIR TOBY

We did keep time, sir, in our catches. Sneck-up!

MALVOLIO

Sir Toby, I must be round with you. My lady bade me
tell you, that, though she harbours you as her kinsman,
she's nothing allied to your disorders. If you can
separate yourself and your misdemeanours, you are
welcome to the house; if not, an it would please you to
take leave of her, she is very willing to bid you farewell.

SIR TOBY [*Beginning another song*]

90 'Farewell, dear heart, since I must needs be gone.'

MARIA

Nay, good Sir Toby.

CLOWN

'His eyes do show his days are almost done.'

MALVOLIO

Is 't even so?

SIR TOBY

'But I will never die.'

CLOWN

Sir Toby, there you lie.

MALVOLIO

This is much credit to you.

---

l. 80 *cosiers'*: cobblers'.   l. 83 *sneck-up*: be hanged!
l. 81 *mitigation*: restraint.   l. 84 *round*: frank.

SIR TOBY

'Shall I bid him go?'

CLOWN

'What an if you do?'

SIR TOBY

'Shall I bid him go, and spare not?'

CLOWN

100 'O, no, no, no, no, you dare not.'

SIR TOBY

Out o' time, sir? ye lie. — Art any more than a steward?
Dost thou think, because thou art virtuous, there shall
be no more cakes and ale?

CLOWN

Yes, by Saint Anne; and ginger shall be hot i' th' mouth
too.

SIR TOBY

Th' art i' th' right. — Go, sir, rub your chain with
crumbs. — A stoup of wine, Maria!

MALVOLIO

Mistress Mary, if you prized my lady's favour at any
thing more than contempt, you would not give means
110 for this uncivil rule: she shall know of it, by this hand.

[*Exit.*

MARIA

Go shake your ears!

SIR ANDREW

'Twere as good a deed as to drink when a man's a-
hungry, to challenge him the field, and then to break
promise with him, and make a fool of him.

---

l. 104 *ginger* (to spice the hot
ale).

l. 106 *rub your chain with
crumbs*: polish your steward's
chain.

SIR TOBY

Do 't, knight: I'll write thee a challenge; or I'll deliver thy indignation to him by word of mouth.

MARIA

Sweet Sir Toby, be patient for to-night...For Monsieur Malvolio, let me alone with him: if I do not gull him into a nayword, and make him a common recreation, do
120 not think I have wit enough to lie straight in my bed: I know I can do it.

SIR TOBY

Possess us, possess us; tell us something of him.

MARIA

Marry, sir, sometimes he is a kind of puritan.

SIR ANDREW

O, if I thought that, I'ld beat him like a dog!

SIR TOBY

What, for being a puritan? thy exquisite reason, dear knight?

SIR ANDREW

I have no exquisite reason for't, but I have reason good enough.

MARIA

The devil a puritan that he is, or any thing constantly,
130 but a time-pleaser; an affection'd ass, that cons state without book, and utters it by great swarths: the best persuaded of himself, so cramm'd, as he thinks, with excellencies, that it is his grounds of faith that all that look on him love him; and on that vice in him will my revenge find notable cause to work.

---

l. 118 *gull*: fool.
l. 119 *nayword*: byword.
l. 122 *possess*: tell.
l. 130 *affection'd*: affected.

l. 130 *cons state without book*: learns polite remarks by heart.
l. 131 *swarths*: sweeps (as of a scythe).

SIR TOBY

What wilt thou do?

MARIA

I will drop in his way some obscure epistles of love; wherein, by the colour of his beard, the shape of his leg, the manner of his gait, the expressure of his eye, 140 forehead, and complexion, he shall find himself most feelingly personated: I can write very like my lady, your niece; on a forgotten matter we can hardly make distinction of our hands.

SIR TOBY

Excellent! I smell a device.

SIR ANDREW

I have 't in my nose too.

SIR TOBY

He shall think, by the letters that thou wilt drop, that they come from my niece, and that she's in love with him.

MARIA

My purpose is, indeed, a horse of that colour.

SIR TOBY

150 And your horse now would make him an ass.

MARIA

Ass, I doubt not.

SIR ANDREW

O, 'twill be admirable!

MARIA

Sport royal, I warrant you: I know my physic will work with him. I will plant you two, and let the fool make a third, where he shall find the letter: observe his

---

l. 141 *personated*: described.
l. 142 *on a forgotten matter*: if the occasion has been forgotten.

l. 151 *Ass* (as!).

construction of it. For this night, to bed, and dream on the event. Farewell.

SIR TOBY

Good night, Penthesilea. [*Exit Maria.*

SIR ANDREW

Before me, she's a good wench.

SIR TOBY

160 She's a beagle, true-bred, and one that adores me: what o' that?

SIR ANDREW

I was adored once too.

SIR TOBY

Let's to bed, knight. — Thou hadst need send for more money.

SIR ANDREW

If I cannot recover your niece, I am a foul way out.

SIR TOBY

Send for money, knight: if thou hast her not i' th' end, call me cut.

SIR ANDREW

If I do not, never trust me, take it how you will.

SIR TOBY

Come, come; I'll go burn some sack; 'tis too late to go
170 to bed now: come, knight; come, knight.

[*Exeunt.*

2

*In the Garden. Enter Sir Toby, Sir Andrew, and Fabian,
a member of the household.*

SIR TOBY

1 COME thy ways, Signior Fabian.

---

l. 158 *Penthesilea*: Queen of the Amazons.
l. 165 *recover*: win.

l. 167 *cut*: cart-horse (slow).
l. 169 *burn*: heat.
l. 169 *sack*: wine.

FABIAN

Nay, I'll come: if I lose a scruple of this sport, let me be boil'd to death with melancholy.

SIR TOBY

Wouldst thou not be glad to have the niggardly rascally sheep-biter come by some notable shame?

FABIAN

I would exult, man: you know he brought me out o' favour with my lady about a bear-baiting here.

SIR TOBY

To anger him, we'll have the bear again; and we will fool him black and blue: — shall we not, Sir Andrew?

SIR ANDREW

10 An we do not, it is pity of our lives.

SIR TOBY

Here comes the little villain.

Enter Maria.

How now, my metal of India!

MARIA

Get ye all three into the box-tree: Malvolio's coming down this walk: he has been yonder i' the sun practising behaviour to his own shadow this half-hour: observe him, for the love of mockery; for I know this letter will make a contemplative idiot of him. Close, in the name of jesting! Lie thou there [*throws down a letter*]; for here comes the trout that must be caught with tickling. [*Exit.*

They hide as Malvolio enters.

MALVOLIO

20 'Tis but fortune; all is fortune! Maria once told me she did affect me: and I have heard herself come thus near, that, should she fancy, it should be one of my complexion. Besides, she uses me with a more exalted

---

l. 5 *sheep-biter*: worrying dog.   l. 21 *affect*: fancy.
l. 12 *metal of India*: gold.

respect than any one else that follows her. What should I think on 't?

SIR TOBY

Here's an overweening rogue!

FABIAN

O, peace! Contemplation makes a rare turkey-cock of him: how he jets under his advanced plumes!

SIR ANDREW

'Slight, I could so beat the rogue!

FABIAN

30 Peace, I say.

MALVOLIO

To be Count Malvolio, —

SIR TOBY

Ah, rogue!

SIR ANDREW

Pistol him, pistol him.

FABIAN

Peace, peace!

MALVOLIO

There is example for 't; the lady of the Strachy married the yeoman of the wardrobe.

SIR ANDREW

Fie on him, Jezebel!

FABIAN

O, peace! now he's deeply in: look how imagination blows him.

MALVOLIO

40 Having been three months married to her, sitting in my state, —

---

l. 28 *jets*: struts.
l. 29 *'slight*: God's light!
l. 35 *the lady of the Strachy married the yeoman of the* *wardrobe* (nothing is known about this affair).
l. 37 *Jezebel* (shameless).
l. 41 *state*: state chair.

SIR TOBY

O, for a stone-bow, to hit him in the eye!

MALVOLIO

Calling my officers about me, in my branch'd velvet gown; having come from a day-bed, where I have left Olivia sleeping, —

SIR TOBY

Fire and brimstone!

FABIAN

O, peace, peace!

MALVOLIO

And then to have the humour of state; and after a demure travel of regard, — telling them I know my place, 50 as I would they should do theirs, — to ask for my kinsman Toby, —

SIR TOBY

Bolts and shackles!

FABIAN

O, peace, peace, peace! now, now.

MALVOLIO

Seven of my people, with an obedient start, make out for him: I frown the while; and perchance wind up my watch, or play with my — some rich jewel. Toby approaches; court'sies there to me, —

SIR TOBY

Shall this fellow live?

FABIAN

Though our silence be drawn from us with cars, yet 60 peace.

---

l. 42 *stone-bow*: cross-bow.
l. 44 *day-bed*: couch.
l. 49: *demure travel of regard*: quiet look round.

l. 56 *play with my — some rich jewel* (he was going to say 'my steward's chain').

MALVOLIO

I extend my hand to him thus, quenching my familia
smile with an austere regard of control, —

SIR TOBY

And does not Toby take you a blow o' the lips, then?

MALVOLIO

Saying, 'Cousin Toby, my fortunes having cast me on
your niece, give me this prerogative of speech,' —

SIR TOBY

What, what?

MALVOLIO

'You must amend your drunkenness.'

SIR TOBY

Out, scab!

FABIAN

Nay, patience, or we break the sinews of our plot.

MALVOLIO

70 'Besides, you waste the treasure of your time with a
foolish knight,' —

SIR ANDREW

That's me, I warrant you.

MALVOLIO

'One Sir Andrew,' —

SIR ANDREW

I knew 'twas I; for many do call me fool.

MALVOLIO

What employment have we here?

[*Taking up the letter.*

SIR TOBY

Now is the woodcock near the gin.

FABIAN

O peace! and the spirit of humours intimate reading
aloud to him!

---

l. 76 *gin*: trap.

MALVOLIO

By my life, this is my lady's hand: these be her very
80 C's, her U's, and her T's; and thus makes she her great
P's. It is, in contempt of question, her hand.

SIR ANDREW

Her C's, her U's, and her T's: why that?

MALVOLIO [*reads*]

'To the unknown beloved, this, and my good wishes':
her very phrases! — By your leave, wax. — Soft! — and
the impressure her Lucrece, with which she uses to
seal: 'tis my lady. To whom should this be?

FABIAN

This wins him, liver and all.

MALVOLIO [*reads*]

'Jove knows I love:
But who?
90 Lips, do not move;
No man must know.'

'No man must know.' — What follows? the numbers
alter'd! — 'No man must know': — if this should be
thee, Malvolio?

SIR TOBY

Marry, hang thee, brock!

MALVOLIO [*reads*]

'I may command where I adore;
But silence, like a Lucrece knife,
With bloodless stroke my heart doth gore:
M, O, A, I, doth sway my life.'

FABIAN

100 A fustian riddle!

---

l. 85 *Lucrece*: a Roman lady.
l. 92 *the numbers alter'd*: a
different metre.
l. 95 *brock*: stinker.

l. 97 *Lucrece* (she took her own
life).
l. 100 *fustian*: nonsensical.

SIR TOBY

Excellent wench, say I.

MALVOLIO

'M, O, A, I, doth sway my life.' — Nay, but first, let
me see, — let me see, — let me see.

FABIAN

What dish o' poison has she dress'd him!

SIR TOBY

And with what wing the staniel checks at it!

MALVOLIO

'I may command where I adore.' Why, she may command me: I serve her; she is my lady. Why, this is
evident to any formal capacity; there is no obstruction
in this: — and the end, — what should that alphabetical
110 position portend? if I could make that resemble something in me, — Softly! — M, O, A, I, —

SIR TOBY

O, ay, make up that: — he is now at a cold scent.

FABIAN

Sowter will cry upon 't, for all this, though it be as
rank as a fox.

MALVOLIO

M, — Malvolio; — M, — why, that begins my name.

FABIAN

Did not I say he would work it out? the cur is excellent
at faults.

MALVOLIO

M, — but then there is no consonancy in the sequel that
suffers under probation: A should follow, but O does.

---

l. 105 *with what wing*: how
quickly.
l. 105 *staniel checks*: hawk flies.
l. 113 *Sowter*: the hound.
l. 114 *rank as a fox* (compared
with the scent of a hare: foxes
were rarely hunted for sport).
l. 118 *no consonancy in the
sequel; that suffers under probation*: what follows doesn't
make sense and can't be
worked out.

FABIAN

120 And O shall end, I hope.

SIR TOBY

Ay, or I'll cudgel him, and make him cry O!

MALVOLIO

And then I comes behind.

FABIAN

Ay, an you had any eye behind you, you might see more
detraction at your heels than fortunes before you.

MALVOLIO

M, O, A, I; — this simulation is not as the former: —
and yet, to crush this a little, it would bow to me, for
every one of these letters are in my name. Soft! here
follows prose. — [*Reads*] 'If this fall into thy hand,
revolve. In my stars I am above thee; but be not afraid
130 of greatness: some are born great, some achieve greatness, and some have greatness thrust upon 'em. Thy
Fates open their hands; let thy blood and spirit embrace
them: and, to inure thyself to what thou art like to be,
cast thy humble slough, and appear fresh. Be opposite
with a kinsman, surly with servants; let thy tongue tang
arguments of state; put thyself into the trick of singularity: she thus advises thee that sighs for thee. Remember who commended thy yellow stockings, and
wish'd to see thee ever cross-garter'd: I say, remember.
140 Go to, thou art made, if thou desirest to be so; if not,
let me see thee a steward still, the fellow of servants,
and not worthy to touch Fortune's fingers. Farewell.

---

l. 124 *detraction*: slander.
l. 125 *simulation*: puzzle.
l. 126 *crush this a little*: work
this out.
l. 126 *bow to*: suit.
l. 129 *revolve*: think deeply.
l. 133 *inure*: accustom.

l. 134 *slough*: skin.
l. 134 *fresh*: eager.
l. 135 *tang arguments of state*:
utter serious matters.
l. 136 *singularity*: individuality.
l. 139 *cross-garter'd* (garters
both above and below knee).

She that would alter services with thee,

THE FORTUNATE-UNHAPPY.'

Daylight and champain discovers not more: this is open.
I will be proud, I will read politic authors, I will baffle
Sir Toby, I will wash off gross acquaintance, I will be
point-devise the very man. I do not now fool myself, to
let imagination jade me; for every reason excites to this,
150 that my lady loves me. She did commend my yellow
stockings of late, she did praise my leg being cross-
garter'd; and in this she manifests herself to my love,
and, with a kind of injunction, drives me to these habits
of her liking. I thank my stars, I am happy. I will be
strange, stout, in yellow stockings, and cross-garter'd,
even with the swiftness of putting on. Jove and my
stars be praised! — Here is yet a postscript. [*Reads*] 'Thou
canst not choose but know who I am. If thou entertain'st
my love, let it appear in thy smiling: thy smiles become
160 thee well; therefore in my presence still smile, dear my
sweet, I prithee.' Jove, I thank thee. — I will smile; I
will do every thing that thou wilt have me.   [*Exit.*

FABIAN

I will not give my part of this sport for a pension of
thousands to be paid from the Sophy.

SIR TOBY

I could marry this wench for this device, —

SIR ANDREW

So could I too.

SIR TOBY

And ask no other dowry with her but such another jest.

---

l. 145 *champain*: open country.   l. 152 *manifests*: shows.
l. 148 *point-devise the very man*:   l. 153 *injunction*: command.
extremely correct.   l. 155 *stout*: proud.
l. 149 *jade*: fool.   l. 164 *Sophy*: Shah of Persia.

SIR ANDREW

Nor I neither.

FABIAN

Here comes my noble gull-catcher.

Enter Maria.

SIR TOBY

170 Wilt thou set thy foot o' my neck?

SIR ANDREW

Or o' mine either?

SIR TOBY

Shall I play my freedom at tray-trip, and become thy bond-slave?

SIR ANDREW

I' faith, or I either?

SIR TOBY

Why, thou hast put him in such a dream, that, when the image of it leaves him, he must run mad.

MARIA

Nay, but say true; does it work upon him?

SIR TOBY

Like aqua-vitæ with a midwife.

MARIA

If you will then see the fruits of the sport, mark his 180 first approach before my lady: he will come to her in yellow stockings, and 'tis a colour she abhors, and cross-garter'd, a fashion she detests; and he will smile upon her, which will now be so unsuitable to her disposition, being addicted to a melancholy as she is, that it cannot but turn him into a notable contempt. If you will see it, follow me.

---

l. 169 *gull*: fool.   l. 178 *aqua-vitæ*: spirits.
l. 172 *tray-trip*: dice.

SIR TOBY

To the gates of Tartar, thou most excellent devil of wit!

SIR ANDREW

I'll make one too.   [*Exeunt.*

Twelfth Night, III. 3 and 5

VERY TRAGICAL MIRTH

*Quince the carpenter and his company of amateur actors, among
whom the dominant personality is Bottom the weaver, hope to
be allowed to present a play at Court to celebrate the wedding
of Theseus, Duke of Athens, and Hippolyta.*

1

*A Room in Quince's House. Enter Quince the Carpenter,
Snug the Joiner, Bottom the Weaver, Flute the Bellows-
mender, Snout the Tinker, and Starveling the Tailor.*

QUINCE

1 Is all our company here?

BOTTOM

You were best to call them generally, man by man,
according to the scrip.

QUINCE

Here is the scroll of every man's name, which is thought
fit, through all Athens, to play in our interlude before
the duke and the duchess on his wedding-day at night.

---

l. 187 *Tartar*: hell.

l. 2 *generally* (he means
'separately').

l. 3 *scrip*: paper.

l. 5 *play*: act.

l. 5 *interlude*: play.

BOTTOM

First, good Peter Quince, say what the play treats on; then read the names of the actors; and so grow to a point.

QUINCE

10 Marry, our play is *The Most Lamentable Comedy and Most Cruel Death of Pyramus and Thisby.*

BOTTOM

A very good piece of work, I assure you, and a merry. — Now, good Peter Quince, call forth your actors by the scroll. — Masters, spread yourselves.

QUINCE

Answer as I call you. — Nick Bottom the weaver.

BOTTOM

Ready. Name what part I am for, and proceed.

QUINCE

You, Nick Bottom, are set down for Pyramus.

BOTTOM

What is Pyramus? a lover, or a tyrant?

QUINCE

A lover, that kills himself most gallant for love.

BOTTOM

20 That will ask some tears in the true performing of it: if I do it, let the audience look to their eyes; I will move storms, I will condole in some measure. To the rest: yet my chief humour is for a tyrant: I could play Ercles rarely, or a part to tear a cat in, to make all split.

> The raging rocks
> And shivering shocks
> Shall break the locks

---

l. 7 *treats on*: is about.   l. 24 *tear a cat*: rage and roar.
l. 23 *Ercles*: Hercules, the Strong Man.

Of prison-gates;
And Phibbus' car
30 Shall shine from far,
And make and mar
The foolish Fates.

This was lofty! — Now name the rest of the players. —
This is Ercles' vein, a tyrant's vein; — a lover is more
condoling.

QUINCE

Francis Flute the bellows-mender.

FLUTE

Here, Peter Quince.

QUINCE

You must take Thisby on you.

FLUTE

What is Thisby? a wandering knight?

QUINCE

40 It is the lady that Pyramus must love.

FLUTE

Nay, faith, let not me play a woman; I have a beard
coming.

QUINCE

That's all one: you shall play it in a mask, and you may
speak as small as you will.

BOTTOM

An I may hide my face, let me play Thisby too: I'll
speak in a monstrous little voice, thisne, thisne: — 'Ah
Pyramus, my lover dear! thy Thisby dear, and lady dear!

QUINCE

No, no; you must play Pyramus: — and, Flute, you
Thisby.

---

l. 29 *Phibbus' car*: the sun's chariot.
l. 34 *vein*: style.

l. 35 *condoling*: sentimental.
l. 46 *thisne, thisne*: like this.

BOTTOM

50 Well, proceed.

QUINCE

Robin Starveling the tailor.

STARVELING

Here, Peter Quince.

QUINCE

Robin Starveling, you must play Thisby's motner. —
Tom Snout the tinker.

SNOUT

Here, Peter Quince.

QUINCE

You, Pyramus' father; myself, Thisby's father; — Snug
the joiner, you, the lion's part: — and, I hope, here is a
play fitted.

SNUG

Have you the lion's part written? pray you, if it be,
60 give it me, for I am slow of study.

QUINCE

You may do it extempore, for it is nothing but roaring.

BOTTOM

Let me play the lion too: I will roar, that I will do any
man's heart good to hear me; I will roar, that I will
make the duke say, 'Let him roar again, let him roar
again.'

QUINCE

An you should do it too terribly, you would fright the
duchess and the ladies, that they would shriek; and that
were enough to hang us all.

ALL

That would hang us, every mother's son.

---

l. 61 *extempore*: without learning it.

BOTTOM

70 I grant you, friends, if you should fright the ladies out of their wits, they would have no more discretion but to hang us: but I will aggravate my voice so, that I will roar you as gently as any sucking dove; I will roar you an 'twere any nightingale.

QUINCE

You can play no part but Pyramus; for Pyramus is a sweet-faced man; a proper man as one shall see in a summer's day; a most lovely, gentleman-like man: therefore you must needs play Pyramus.

BOTTOM

Well, I will undertake it. What beard were I best to
80 play it in?

QUINCE

Why, what you will ... But, masters, here are your parts: and I am to entreat you, request you, and desire you, to con them by to-morrow night; and meet me in the palace wood, a mile without the town, by moonlight: there will we rehearse, for if we meet in the city, we shall be dogg'd with company, and our devices known. In the mean time I will draw a bill of properties, such as our play wants. I pray you, fail me not.

BOTTOM

We will meet; and there we may rehearse most obscenely
90 and courageously.

QUINCE

Take pains; be perfit: adieu. At the duke's oak we meet.

BOTTOM

Enough!

---

l. 72 *aggravate*: exaggerate (but he means the opposite).

l. 89 *obscenely* (he thinks that it means that they can be seen).

In the Palace Wood. Enter Quince, Snug, Bottom, Flute, Snout, and Starveling.

BOTTOM

1   ARE we all met?

QUINCE

Pat, pat; and here's a marvellous convenient place for our rehearsal. This green plot shall be our stage, this hawthorn-brake our tiring-house; and we will do it in action as we will do it before the duke.

BOTTOM

Peter Quince, —

QUINCE

What say'st thou, bully Bottom?

BOTTOM

There are things in this comedy of *Pyramus and Thisby* that will never please. First, Pyramus must draw a
10   sword to kill himself; which the ladies cannot abide. How answer you that?

SNOUT

By'r lakin, a parlous fear!

STARVELING

I believe we must leave the killing out, when all is done.

BOTTOM

Not a whit: I have a device to make all well. Write me a prologue; and let the prologue seem to say, we will do no harm with our swords, and that Pyramus is not kill'd indeed; and, for the more better assurance, tell them that I Pyramus am not Pyramus, but Bottom the weaver: this will put them out of fear.

---

l. 7 *bully* (something like our phrase 'good old').

l. 12 *by'r lakin*: by Our Lady!

l. 12 *parlous*: perilous.

QUINCE

20 Well, we will have such a prologue; and it shall be written in eight and six.

BOTTOM

No, make it two more: let it be written in eight and eight.

SNOUT

Will not the ladies be afeard of the lion?

STARVELING

I fear it, I promise you.

BOTTOM

Masters, you ought to consider with yourselves: to bring in, — God shield us! — a lion among ladies is a most dreadful thing; for there is not a more fearful wild-fowl than your lion living; and we ought to look to 't.

SNOUT

Therefore another prologue must tell he is not a lion.

BOTTOM

30 Nay, you must name his name, and half his face must be seen through the lion's neck; and he himself must speak through, saying thus, or to the same defect, — 'Ladies,' — or, 'Fair ladies, — I would wish you,' — or, 'I would request you,' — or, 'I would entreat you, — not to fear, not to tremble: my life for yours. If you think I come hither as a lion, it were pity of my life: no, I am no such thing; I am a man as other men are': — and there, indeed, let him name his name, and tell them plainly he is Snug the joiner.

QUINCE

40 Well, it shall be so. But there is two hard things, — that is, to bring the moonlight into a chamber; for, you know, Pyramus and Thisby meet by moonlight.

---

l. 21 *eight and six* (stresses in the lines).

SNUG

Doth the moon shine that night we play our play?

BOTTOM

A calendar, a calendar! look in the almanac; find out moonshine, find out moonshine.

QUINCE

Yes, it doth shine that night.

BOTTOM

Why, then may you leave a casement of the great chamber-window, where we play, open, and the moon may shine in at the casement.

QUINCE

50 Ay; or else one must come in with a bush of thorns and a lantern, and say he comes to disfigure, or to present, the person of moonshine. Then, there is another thing: we must have a wall in the great chamber; for Pyramus and Thisby, says the story, did talk through the chink of a wall.

SNUG

You can never bring in a wall. — What say you, Bottom?

BOTTOM

Some man or other must present wall: and let him have some plaster, or some loam, or some rough-cast about him, to signify wall; and let him hold his fingers thus, 60 and through that cranny shall Pyramus and Thisby whisper.

QUINCE

If that may be, then all is well. Come, sit down, every mother's son, and rehearse your parts. Pyramus, you begin: when you have spoken your speech, enter into that brake; — and so every one according to his cue.

Enter Puck* behind.

---

* A 'knavish sprite'.

PUCK

What hempen home-spuns have we swaggering here,
So near the cradle of the fairy queen?
What, a play toward! I'll be an auditor;
An actor too perhaps, if I see cause.

QUINCE

70 Speak, Pyramus. — Thisby, stand forth.

BOTTOM

Thisby, the flowers of odious savours sweet, —

QUINCE

Odours, odours.

BOTTOM

—— odours savours sweet:
So hath thy breath, my dearest Thisby dear. —
But hark, a voice! stay thou but here awhile,
And by and by I will to thee appear.   [*Exit.*

PUCK [*aside*]

A stranger Pyramus than e'er play'd here.   [*Exit.*

FLUTE

Must I speak now?

QUINCE

Ay, marry, must you; for you must understand he goes
but to see a noise that he heard, and is to come again.

FLUTE

80 Most radiant Pyramus, most lily-white of hue,
    Of colour like the red rose on triumphant brier,
Most brisky juvenal, and eke most lovely Jew,
    As true as truest horse, that yet would never tire,
I'll meet thee, Pyramus, at Ninny's tomb.

QUINCE

'Ninus' tomb,' man: — why, you must not speak that

---

l. 66 *hempen home-spuns*: coarse
fellows.

176

yet; that you answer to Pyramus: you speak all your part
at once, cues and all. — Pyramus, enter: your cue is past;
it is, 'never tire.'

FLUTE

O, — As true as truest horse, that yet would never tire.
*Enter Puck, and Bottom with a donkey's head instead of his own.**

BOTTOM

90 If I were fair, Thisby, I were only thine: —

QUINCE

O monstrous! O strange! we are haunted. —
Pray, masters! fly, masters! — Help!
         [Exit with Snug, Flute, Snout, and Starveling.

PUCK

I'll follow you, I'll lead you about a round,
   Through bog, through bush, through brake, through
      brier:
Sometime a horse I'll be, sometime a hound,
   A hog, a headless bear, sometime a fire;
And neigh, and bark, and grunt, and roar, and burn,
Like horse, hound, hog, bear, fire, at every turn.
                      [Exit.

BOTTOM

Why do they run away? this is a knavery of them to make
100 me afeard.

Enter Snout.

SNOUT

O Bottom, thou art chang'd! what do I see on thee?

BOTTOM

What do you see? you see an ass-head of your own, do
you?   *[Exit Snout.*

Enter Quince.

---

* he has been enchanted by   l. 102 *of your own*: like yours.
Puck.

QUINCE

Bless thee, Bottom! bless thee! thou art translated.

[*Exit.*

BOTTOM

I see their knavery: this is to make an ass of me; to
fright me, if they could. But I will not stir from this
place, do what they can: I will walk up and down here,
and I will sing, that they shall hear I am not afraid.

[*Sings.*

  The ousel-cock so black of hue,
110   With orange-tawny bill,
  The throstle with his note so true,
   The wren with little quill.

3

At Court.

THESEUS

1 COME now; what masks, what dances shall we have,
To wear away this long age of three hours
Between our after-supper and bed-time?
Where is our usual manager of mirth?
What revels are in hand? Is there no play,
To ease the anguish of a torturing hour?
Call Philostrate.

PHILOSTRATE

  Here, mighty Theseus.

THESEUS

Say, what abridgement have you for this evening?
What mask? what music? How shall we beguile
10 The lazy time, if not with some delight?

PHILOSTRATE

There is a brief how many sports are ripe:

---

l. 11 *brief*: list.   l. 11 *ripe*: ready.

Make choice of which your highness will see first ...
> [*Giving a paper.*

THESEUS [*reads*]
'A tedious brief scene of young Pyramus
And his love Thisbe; very tragical mirth.'
Merry and tragical! tedious and brief!
That is, hot ice and wondrous strange snow.
How shall we find the concord of this discord?

PHILOSTRATE
A play there is, my lord, some ten words long,
Which is as brief as I have known a play;
20 But by ten words, my lord, it is too long,
Which makes it tedious; for in all the play
There is not one word apt, one player fitted:
And tragical, my noble lord, it is;
For Pyramus therein doth kill himself.
Which, when I saw rehears'd, I must confess,
Made mine eyes water, but more merry tears
The passion of loud laughter never shed.

THESEUS
What are they that do play it?

PHILOSTRATE
Hard-handed men, that work in Athens here,
30 Which never labour'd in their minds till now;
And now have toil'd their unbreath'd memories
With this same play, against your nuptial.

THESEUS
And we will hear it.

PHILOSTRATE
No, my noble lord;
It is not for you: I have heard it over,
And it is nothing, nothing in the world;

---

l. 31 *unbreath'd*: unpractised.

Unless you can find sport in their intents,
Extremely stretch'd and conn'd with cruel pain,
To do you service.

THESEUS

        I will hear that play;
For never any thing can be amiss,
40 When simpleness and duty tender it.
Go, bring them in: — and take your places, ladies.

PHILOSTRATE

So please your grace, the Prologue is address'd.

THESEUS

Let him approach.   [*Flourish of trumpets.*
                 Enter the Prologue.

PROLOGUE*

If we offend, it is with our good will.
    That you should think, we come not to offend,
But with good will. To show our simple skill,
    That is the true beginning of our end.
Consider then, we come but in despite.
    We do not come, as minding to content you,
50 Our true intent is. All for your delight,
    We are not here. That you should here repent you,
The actors are at hand; and, by their show,
You shall know all that you are like to know, —

THESEUS

This fellow doth not stand upon points.

LYSANDER

He hath rid his prologue like a rough colt; he knows not
the stop. A good moral, my lord: it is not enough to
speak, but to speak true.

---

l. 37 *conn'd*: learnt.
l. 42 *address'd*: ready.
* The actor has paid no atten-
tion to the stops.

l. 48 *despite*: ill will.
l. 54 *stand upon points*: bother
about the stops.

HIPPOLYTA

Indeed he hath play'd on his prologue like a child on a
recorder; a sound, but not in government.

THESEUS

60 His speech was like a tangled chain; nothing impair'd,
but all disorder'd. Who is next?
Enter Pyramus and Thisbe, Wall, Moonshine, and Lion.

PROLOGUE

Gentles, perchance you wonder at this show;
 But wonder on, till truth make all things plain.
This man is Pyramus, if you would know;
 This beauteous lady, Thisbe is certain.
This man, with lime and rough-cast, doth present
 Wall, that vile Wall which did these lovers sunder;
And through Wall's chink, poor souls, they are content
 To whisper; at the which let no man wonder.
70 This man, with lantern, dog, and bush of thorn,
 Presenteth Moonshine; for, if you will know
By moonshine did these lovers think no scorn
 To meet at Ninus' tomb, there, there to woo.
This grisly beast, which by name Lion hight,
The trusty Thisbe, coming first by night,
Did scare away, or rather did affright;
And, as she fled, her mantle she did fall,
 Which Lion vile with bloody mouth did stain.
Anon comes Pyramus, sweet youth and tall,
80 And finds his trusty Thisbe's mantle slain:
Whereat, with blade, with bloody blameful blade,
 He bravely broach'd his boiling bloody breast;
And Thisbe, tarrying in mulberry shade,
 His dagger drew, and died. For all the rest,
Let Lion, Moonshine, Wall, and lovers twain,

---

l. 59 *recorder*: flute.   l. 74 *hight*: is called.
l. 60 *impair'd*: damaged.

At large discourse, while here they do remain.

[Exeunt Prologue, Pyramus, Thisbe, Lion,
and Moonshine.

THESEUS

I wonder if the lion be to speak.

DEMETRIUS

No wonder, my lord: one lion may, when many asses do.

WALL

In this same interlude it doth befall
90 That I, one Snout by name, present a wall;
And such a wall, as I would have you think,
That had in it a crannied hole or chink,
Through which the lovers, Pyramus and Thisbe,
Did whisper often very secretly.
This loam, this rough-çast, and this stone, doth show
That I am that same wall; the truth is so:
And this the cranny is, right and sinister,
Through which the fearful lovers are to whisper.

THESEUS

Would you desire lime and hair to speak better?

DEMETRIUS

100 It is the wittiest partition that ever I heard discourse,
my lord.

THESEUS

Pyramus draws near the wall: silence!

Enter Pyramus.

PYRAMUS

O grim-look'd night! O night with hue so black!
  O night, which ever art when day is not!
O night, O night! alack, alack, alack,
  I fear my Thisbe's promise is forgot! —

---

l. 97 *sinister*: left.

And thou, O wall, O sweet, O lovely wall,
    That stand'st between her father's ground and mine!
Thou wall, O wall, O sweet and lovely wall,
110   Show me thy chink, to blink through with mine eyne!
                    [Wall holds up his fingers.
Thanks, courteous wall: Jove shield thee well for this!
    But what see I? No Thisbe do I see.
O wicked wall, through whom I see no bliss!
    Curst be thy stones for thus deceiving me!

THESEUS

The wall, methinks, being sensible, should curse again.

BOTTOM

No, in truth, sir, he should not. 'Deceiving me' is
Thisbe's cue: she is to enter now, and I am to spy her
through the wall. You shall see, it will fall pat as I told
you. — Yonder she comes.

Enter Thisbe.

THISBE

120 O wall, full often hast thou heard my moans,
    For parting my fair Pyramus and me!
My cherry lips have often kiss'd thy stones,
    Thy stones with lime and hair knit up in thee.

PYRAMUS

I see a voice: now will I to the chink,
To spy an I can hear my Thisbe's face. —
Thisbe!

THISBE

My love! thou art my love, I think.

PYRAMUS

Think what thou wilt, I am thy lover's grace;
And, like Limander, am I trusty still.

---

l. 115 *sensible*: a person.   l. 129   *Limander*: Leander,
                                      Hero's lover.

THISBE

130 And I like Helen, till the Fates me kill.

PYRAMUS

Not Shafalus to Procrus was so true.

THISBE

As Shafalus to Procrus, I to you.

PYRAMUS

O, kiss me through the hole of this vile wall!

THISBE

I kiss the wall's hole, not your lips at all.

PYRAMUS

Wilt thou at Ninny's tomb meet me straightway?

THISBE

'Tide life, 'tide death, I come without delay.

               [*Exeunt Pyramus and Thisbe.*

WALL

Thus have I, wall, my part discharged so;

And, being done, thus wall away doth go.   [*Exit.*

THESEUS

Now is the mural down between the two neighbours.

DEMETRIUS

140 No remedy, my lord, when walls are so wilful to hear without warning.

HIPPOLYTA

This is the silliest stuff that e'er I heard.

THESEUS

The best in this kind are but shadows: and the worst are no worse, if imagination amend them.

HIPPOLYTA

It must be your imagination then, and not theirs.

THESEUS

If we imagine no worse of them than they of themselves,

---

l. 130 *Helen*: Hero.   l. 131 *Procrus*: Procris.
l. 131 *Shafalus*: Cephalus.   l. 143 *in*: of.

they may pass for excellent men. — Here come two noble
beasts in, a moon and a lion.

Enter Lion and Moonshine.

LION

You, ladies, you, whose gentle hearts do fear,
150   The smallest monstrous mouse that creeps on floor,
May now perchance both quake and tremble here,
    When lion rough in wildest rage doth roar.
Then know that I, as Snug the joiner am
No lion fell, nor else no lion's dam;
For, if I should as lion come in strife
Into this place, 'twere pity on my life.

THESEUS

A very gentle beast, and of a good conscience.

DEMETRIUS

The very best at a beast, my lord, that e'er I saw.

LYSANDER

This lion is a very fox for his valour.

THESEUS

160 True; and a goose for his discretion.

DEMETRIUS

Not so, my lord; for his valour cannot carry his discretion; and the fox carries the goose.

THESEUS

His discretion, I am sure, cannot carry his valour; for the
goose carries not the fox. It is well: leave it to his
discretion, and let us listen to the moon …

MOONSHINE

This lantern doth the horned moon present;
Myself the man-i-th'-moon do seem to be.

THESEUS

This is the greatest error of all the rest: the man should
be put into the lantern. How is it else the man-i'-th'-
170 moon?

DEMETRIUS

He dares not come there for the candle; for, you see, it is already in snuff.

HIPPOLYTA

I am a-weary of this moon: would he would change!

THESEUS

It appears, by his small light of discretion, that he is in the wane; but yet, in courtesy, in all reason, we must stay the time.

LYSANDER

Proceed, moon.

MOONSHINE

All that I have to say is, to tell you that the lantern is the moon; I, the man-i'-th'-moon; this thorn-bush, my 180 thorn-bush; and this dog, my dog.

DEMETRIUS

Why, all these should be in the lantern; for all these are in the moon. But, silence! here comes Thisbe.

Enter Thisbe.

THISBE

This is old Ninny's tomb. Where is my love?

[*The Lion roars; Thisbe runs off.*

DEMETRIUS

Well roar'd, lion.

THESEUS

Well run, Thisbe.

HIPPOLYTA

Well shone, moon. — Truly, the moon shines with a good grace. [*The Lion tears Thisbe's mantle, and exit.*

THESEUS

Well mous'd, lion.

---

l. **172** *in snuff*: flaring.

DEMETRIUS

And then came Pyramus.

LYSANDER

190 And so the lion vanish'd.

Enter Pyramus.

PYRAMUS

Sweet moon, I thank thee for thy sunny beams;
    I thank thee, moon, for shining now so bright;
For, by thy gracious, golden, glittering streams,
    I trust to taste of truest Thisbe's sight.
                    But stay, — O spite! —
                    But mark, poor knight,
                    What dreadful dole is here!
                    Eyes, do you see?
                    How can it be?
200   O dainty duck! O dear!
                    Thy mantle good,
                    What, stain'd with blood?
                    Approach, ye Furies fell!
                    O fates, come, come,
                    Cut thread and thrum;
                    Quail, crush, conclude, and quell!

THESEUS

This passion, and the death of a dear friend, would go
near to make a man look sad.

HIPPOLYTA

Beshrew my heart, but I pity the man.

PYRAMUS

210 O, wherefore, Nature, didst thou lions frame?
    Since lion vile hath here deflower'd my dear:
Which is — no, no — which was the fairest dame

---

l. 203 *Furies*: avenging goddesses.
l. 203 *fell*: fierce.

l. 205 *thread and thrum*: the
thread of life.

That liv'd, that lov'd, that lik'd, that look'd with cheer.
       Come, tears, confound;
       Out, sword, and wound
The pap of Pyramus, —
       Ay, that left pap,
       Where heart doth hop: —
                          [Stabs himself.

Thus die I, thus, thus, thus.
220   Now am I dead,
       Now am I fled;
My soul is in the sky:
       Tongue, lose thy light;
       Moon, take thy flight: —
                        [Exit Moonshine.
       Now die, die, die, die, die.   *[Dies.*

DEMETRIUS

No die, but an ace, for him; for he is but one.

LYSANDER

Less than an ace, man; for he is dead; he is nothing.

THESEUS

With the help of a surgeon he might yet recover; and prove an ass.

HIPPOLYTA

230 How chance Moonshine is gone before Thisbe comes back to find her lover?

THESEUS

She will find him by starlight. — Here she comes, and her passion ends the play.

Enter Thisbe.

HIPPOLYTA

Methinks she should not use a long one for such a Pyramus: I hope she will be brief.

---

l. 226 *die*: dice.   l. 226 *one*: unique.

DEMETRIUS

A mote will turn the balance, which Pyramus, which
Thisbe, is the better; he for a man, God warrant us, —
she for a woman, God bless us.

LYSANDER

She hath spied him already with those sweet eyes.

DEMETRIUS

240 And thus she moans:

THISBE

    Asleep, my love?
      What, dead, my dove?
    O Pyramus, arise!
      Speak, speak. Quite dumb?
      Dead, dead? A tomb
    Must cover thy sweet eyes.
      These lily lips,
      This cherry nose,
    These yellow cowslip cheeks,
250   Are gone, are gone:
      Lovers, make moan:
    His eyes were green as leeks.
      O Sisters Three,
      Come, come to me,
    With hands as pale as milk;
      Lay them in gore,
      Since you have shore
    With shears his thread of silk.
      Tongue, not a word:
260   Come, trusty sword;
    Come, blade, my breast imbrue;

                    [*Stabs herself.*

    And, farewell, friends, —

---

l. 236 *mote*: speck.   l. 257 *shore*: cut.
l. 253 *Sisters Three*: The Fates.

Thus Thisbe ends, —
Adieu, adieu, adieu.   [*Dies.*

THESEUS

Moonshine and Lion are left to bury the dead.

DEMETRIUS

Ay, and Wall too.

BOTTOM

No, I assure you; the wall is down that parted their
fathers. Will it please you to see the epilogue, or to hear
a Bergomask dance between two of our company?

THESEUS

270 No epilogue, I pray you; for your play needs no excuse.
Never excuse; for when the players are all dead, there
need none to be blamed. Marry, if he that writ it had
play'd Pyramus and hang'd himself in Thisbe's garter,
it would have been a fine tragedy: and so it is, truly; and
very notably discharg'd. But, come, your Bergomask:
let your epilogue alone.   [*A dance.*
The iron tongue of midnight hath told twelve: —
Lovers, to bed; 'tis almost fairy-time.
I fear we shall out-sleep the coming morn,
280 As much as we this night have overwatch'd.
This palpable-gross play hath well beguil'd
The heavy gait of night. — Sweet friends, to bed. —
A fortnight hold we this solemnity
In nightly revels and new jollity.   [*Exeunt.*
                    Enter Puck.

PUCK

Now the hungry lion roars,
    And the wolf behowls the moon;
Whilst the heavy ploughman snores,
    All with weary task fordone.

---

l. 269 *Bergomask*:   country
dance.

Now the wasted brands do glow,
 Whilst the screech-owl, screeching loud,
Puts the wretch that lies in woe
 In remembrance of a shroud.
Now it is the time of night,
 That the graves, all gaping wide,
Every one lets forth his sprite,
 In the church-way paths to glide:
And we fairies, that do run
 By the triple Hecate's team
From the presence of the sun,
 Following darkness like a dream,
Now are frolic: not a mouse
Shall disturb this hallow'd house:
I am sent, with broom, before,
To sweep the dust behind the door.

Enter Oberon and Titania, King and Queen of the Fairies, with their Train.

OBERON

Through the house give glimmering light,
 By the dead and drowsy fire;
Every elf and fairy sprite
 Hop as light as bird from brier;
And this ditty, after me,
Sing, and dance it trippingly.

TITANIA

First, rehearse your song by rote,
To each word a warbling note:
Hand in hand, with fairy grace,
Will we sing, and bless this place.
       [Song and dance.

---

l. 298 *Hecate*: Queen of the Night. l. 311 *by rote*: from memory.

OBERON

Now, until the break of day,
Through this house each fairy stray.
To the best bride-bed will we,
Which by us shall blessed be;
And the issue there create
Ever shall be fortunate.
So shall all the couples three
Ever true in loving be ...
With this field-dew consecrate,
Every fairy take his gait;
And each several chamber bless,
Through this palace, with sweet peace:
And the owner of it, blest,
Ever shall in safety rest.
    Trip away:
    Make no stay;
Meet me all by break of day.

A Midsummer-Night's Dream, II. 1, III. 1, V. 1